ALEXANDRA MIK
was a Russian revol
October Revolution,
Social Welfare. Her dipi...
was appointed Soviet Ambassador to Norway, ..
second woman in the world to hold such a high diplomatic post
in modern times. She also served as Ambassador to Mexico and
Sweden. She was a member of the Soviet delegation to the
League of Nations. She wrote numerous essays and theoretical
tracts, as well as two novels, *The Love of Worker Bees*
and *Red Love*.

PARVATHI MENON trained as a historian,
and recently retired as a journalist with *The Hindu* group.

Коллонтай

The

Soviet

Woman

# Alexandra

# Kollontai

The

Soviet

Woman

*Selected*

*Essays*

Introduction by Parvathi Menon

Offset edition first published in October 2017
Digital print edition, January 2020

LeftWord Books
2254/2A Shadi Khampur
New Ranjit Nagar
New Delhi 110008
INDIA

LeftWord Books is the publishing division of
Naya Rasta Publishers Pvt. Ltd.

leftword.com

ISBN 978-93-80118-63-5

# CONTENTS

# INTRODUCTION
Parvathi Menon

Alexandra Kollontai (1872-1952) was an inspiring figure of the Bolshevik Revolution of 1917 whose revolutionary legacy slipped into relative obscurity in the decades following her death. Some of her sister revolutionaries – Rosa Luxemburg, Clara Zetkin and Nadezhda Krupskaya, for example – became celebrated household names, and their ideas and writings form a well-known part of the intellectual inheritance of socialism for left and women's movements worldwide. There was a brief swell of interest in Kollontai in the feminist movement of the 1970s and 1980s, with some projecting her as a tragic representative of the failures of socialism, and others casting her as a victim of a patriarchal Bolshevik state apparatus that suppressed her work and writing.

The first serious biographies in English of Kollontai were published in 1979-80.[1] Despite the contributions of these studies, the extraordinary life and times of Alexandra Kollontai remain, at best, of niche academic and political interest today. What are the reasons for this? Why is it that the life and work of Kollontai are less known than that of many of her peers? Her writings, after all, are voluminous. She wrote on politics, Marxist theory, country-specific economic studies and the women's question. She left letters, diaries, memoirs and pamphlets, theoretical tracts, articles and creative literature. She wrote two novels – *The Love of Worker Bees* and *Red Love* – and several short stories, in which her theories and views on love, sexuality and socialist morality found expression through fictional characters.

One reason advanced by commentators for Kollontai's relative

[1] Barbara Evans Clements, *Bolshevik Feminist: The Life of Aleksandra Kollontai*, Bloomington: Indiana University Press, 1979; Cathy Porter, *Alexandra Kollontai: A Biography*, London: Virago Press, 1980.

obscurity in her lifetime is that she was sidelined by the socialist establishment for being too much of a libertine when it came to matters of love, sexuality and marriage. In fact, several contemporary critics saw her as a thinly disguised advocate of promiscuity or 'free love', and therefore an unpredictable or even dangerous influence. The 'glass of water' theory of sexuality that is attributed to her – namely, that sex is as commonplace and necessary as a glass of water to those who are thirsty – is a contextually misplaced reading of her arguments on sexuality, yet it has stuck.

Kollontai was resolutely opposed to bourgeois feminism: a form of feminism that was anti-Marxist and driven by an agenda of free love. At the same time, she was one of a small group of male and female communists of her time who engaged intellectually with the issue of sexual morality in the context of women's liberation. She perhaps took the analysis of the sexual aspect of the women's question further than most. She envisioned the possibilities of women's freedom as tied to a socialist future, and set out the mechanisms by which women's subordination – political and economic, of course, but equally in terms of ideas and attitudes – could, and should, be done away with under socialism.

Kollontai travelled outside the Soviet Union for the first time in 1922, as a member of a trade delegation to Norway. Her appointment as the Soviet Ambassador to Norway a couple of years later, in 1924, marked the beginning of a long, illustrious and insufficiently studied diplomatic career. Her forthright and radical views, and strong personality may not have been to the liking of conservatives in the Bolshevik party, but it is wrong to assume that her feminism was the reason for her transfer from the party headquarters to the arena of Soviet foreign policy. This is but an easy explanation that avoids coming to grips with the complex interplay of political and class tendencies among the highly talented Bolshevik leaders of that period of revolutionary upheaval.

Kollontai was a charismatic mass leader and a senior Bolshevik functionary who participated in the overthrow of the tsarist regime and the establishment of a socialist state. She was the first and only woman to be elected to the Central Committee of the Bolshevik party in 1917. She was one of twelve senior Bolsheviks to attend the historic meeting of 24th October that year, at which the decision was taken to launch an armed uprising and storm the winter palace. As the first woman Commissar she was given charge of the Department of Social Welfare, and she was instrumental in drafting several early welfare legislations. While the status of women and their political education may have been the focus of her politics, she always maintained that this task was contingent on the political overthrow of tsarism and the establishment of a new revolutionary state. Any attempt, therefore, to marginalize Kollontai's work on the grounds that it was chiefly concerned with women's issues is to mirror the very sexism that she sought to undermine.

FOUR PHASES

We can gain an understanding of the various factors that influenced Kollontai by dividing her life into four broad phases. The first phase extends from her birth, in March 1872, into a wealthy bourgeois family in St. Petersburg, to 1898, when she went to Zurich to study Marxist economics, leaving behind her husband and young son. This break with her family marked the beginning of her life as a political activist.

The second phase, which stretches roughly from 1899 to 1910, was a period of consolidation of Kollontai's Marxist convictions and saw her establishing contact with some of the leading European revolutionaries of that time. She attended the Seventh International Socialist Congress in Stuttgart and the First International Conference of Socialist Women, where she was the only Russian delegate, in 1907. The following year she wrote *Social Basis of the Women's Question*, outlining the socialist approach to the women's liberation movement. In 1910 she addressed the Eighth Socialist Congress held in Copenhagen and the Second Conference of

Socialist Women. Kollontai thus was politically active in this phase of her life, but ideologically uncertain. She participated in the Russian revolution of 1905 (which was crushed by the tsarist state); joined the Mensheviks the following year; was then forced to flee Russia and go to Berlin, where she became a member of the German Social Democratic Party (SDP).

The third phase of Kollontai's life, from 1911 to 1922, saw her embracing Bolshevik politics. She travelled across Europe and the United States of America mobilizing support for the Russian revolutionary cause and against the war. In March 1917 she learnt of the revolution in Russia, the Tsar's abdication and the formation of the provisional government. That same month she established contact for the first time with Lenin, who asked her to carry his Letters from Afar to Russia, to be published in *Pravda*. In April she returned to Russia and was elected as a delegate to the Petrograd Soviet. In April again, she joined the small band of comrades that met Lenin on his return from Switzerland. Kollontai was one among a few who backed Lenin's *April Theses*, and she threw herself into the revolutionary campaign preceding October 1917: she addressed meetings in factories, on the streets and even on battleships, speaking in support of the Bolshevik programme and calling for the overthrow of the provisional government. She wrote articles for the Bolshevik women's paper, *Rabotnitsa*. At the first All-Russian Trade Union Congress held that June, she urged unions to address the demands and needs of women workers. In July she was arrested and imprisoned by the provisional government as a German spy, but was nevertheless elected in absentia to the Bolshevik Central Committee. She was released from prison in early September but put under house arrest, from which she was freed only later that month.

By this time Kollontai was very much at the heart of political action in Petrograd, the Bolshevik headquarters. She attended the historic Central Committee meeting that planned the armed insurrection which overthrew the Kerensky government and brought the Bolsheviks to power. She was elected Commissar of Social Welfare in November 1917, and, at the First Conference of Petrograd Working Women, she introduced a new Bolshevik legislation on maternity protection. Early the following year she presented the new Marriage Law, which was passed by the Bolshevik government.

Kollontai was one of a group of senior Bolsheviks who opposed Lenin in his support of the Brest-Litovsk Treaty with Germany, which ended Russia's participation in the First World War. She spoke against the terms of the treaty at the Fourth Congress of Soviets in March 1918, at which it was ratified,[2] and resigned from the party Commissariat in protest. In September 1919 she joined the new Women's Department, the Zhenotdel, and in 1920 became its Director. She now distanced herself from the Bolsheviks and joined the Workers' Opposition group, led by Alexander Shlyapnikov, in 1921.[3] Workers' Opposition was attacked by the Bolshevik delegates as a left-adventurist deviation at both the 10th and 11th Party Congresses, and Kollontai herself came under sustained criticism, both for her political views and lack of discipline in her private life, and was threatened with expulsion.[4] By early 1922 Stalin had taken over as general secretary of the party, and Lenin suffered his first stroke. Kollontai was sent away to Odessa in disgrace. That summer, however, Stalin recalled her to Moscow and offered her a diplomatic post. She left for Oslo, Norway, as part of a Soviet trade delegation.

---

[2] Porter, *Alexandra Kollontai*, pp. 289-91. Kollontai was in agreement with those who felt that the treaty, with its harsh terms, should not be signed, and that the Soviet Union should wait and aid the Austrian and German proletariat to overthrow the ruling classes of the two countries – an event they believed was imminent. For Lenin, however, protection of the newly created Soviet stage was of paramount importance, and peace at the borders was essential for this to happen.

[3] Ibid., p. 342.

[4] Ibid., pp. 362-64. Also see, Beatrice Brodsky Farnsworth, 'Bolshevism, the Woman Question, and Aleksandra Kollontai', *The American Historical Review*, Vol. 81, No. 2 (April 1976), pp. 292-316.

Throughout this phase of her life Kollontai wrote copiously and spoke from public platforms on the women's question. Her writings of this period include a 1913 essay titled 'The New Woman'; a book, *Society and Motherhood*, published in Russia in 1916; several articles in *Rabotnitsa*; and the essay 'Communism and the Family', based on her speech at the First All-Russian Congress of Working and Peasant Women. Her lectures included a series of talks at Sverdlov University on communist morality and on women in the economy. It was also a period of ill health for her. She suffered a heart attack in early 1919, and was ill in the winter months with typhus, septicemia, nephritis and heart-related problems.

The last phase of Kollontai's life, from 1924 till her death in March 1952, encompassed her diplomatic career and her return to Russia upon retirement. These years marked a decisive break for her. She was more or less cut off from domestic politics, and from her involvement with crafting and executing policies for women in the Soviet Union. She was now a diplomat, and she adjusted herself to the new task of representing her socialist government abroad. She spent most of the years of her diplomatic career in Norway and Sweden, but she also had a stint in Mexico in 1926-27 as Ambassador for the Soviet Union. She maintained close ties with Finland – the country of origin of her maternal grandfather – and was instrumental in negotiating a peace treaty with Finland and Sweden to secure their break with Hitler in 1944, during the Second World War. In a practical sense, Kollontai's successes in diplomacy exceeded the wins she had garnered as a politician and advocate of women's rights. Indeed, despite the lashings she received from several contemporaries, both within and outside the party, for her radical views on women and sexuality, she was awarded the Order of Lenin in 1933 in recognition of her work and contributions for the cause of women, and was nominated to the Nobel Peace Prize in 1945.

Kollontai escaped Stalin's purges of the 1930s. For this too she has been criticized, with her detractors alleging that political opportunism impelled her to shut her eyes to the deportations and deaths of close friends and political associates. At least one of her biographers has however tried to understand Kollontai's response to the situation at that time in Russia, and the actions of the government under Stalin, as driven by political conviction and not opportunism.[5] Kollontai genuinely believed that the transition to socialism would be a fraught one. In a personal memoir published on the occasion of the 15th Party Congress (1932), she wrote an anecdotal account, entitled 'Days of October', of the historic Central Committee meeting of 1917 that she had attended at which plans were made for the seizure of power. The article was republished on the occasion of the 20th Party Congress in 1937. However, in this second version the article was rewritten (by official censors, it is presumed), such that Kollontai's original recall of the spirit of comradeship that prevailed at that important meeting was twisted and transformed into an account of 'traitors' (Trotsky, Kamenev and Zinoviev) plotting against Lenin and the socialist state.[6] Despite all this, Kollontai believed in and supported the socialist experiment that was taking place in the Soviet Union, and was confident that the country would survive its trial by fire. She in fact criticized the United Opposition that she herself had been a part of:

> If it sees faults in the Party now, who if not its leaders were responsible for these faults in the first place? People's memory is not so short. From what the Oppositionists say, one would think the policies of the party and the structure of the apparatus only became corrupt at the moment they broke with it.[7]

---

[5] Cathy Porter's biography is sympathetic to Kollontai, and offers a more complex and nuanced set of reasons for her having escaped the purges. See Porter, *Alexandra Kollontai*, pp. 388-89, 403, Chapter Nineteen: 'The Purges, Fascism and War'.

[6] Ibid., p. 426.

[7] Ibid., p. 428.

During the sweep of Stalin's purges, Kollontai too expected to be summoned to Moscow and tried, according to her biographer. She looked for a rationale behind the purges, comparing them to the persecution of heretics during the Renaissance. She wrote:

> I can understand that era [of the Renaissance] better now. What persecution of ideas there was, and what a will to defend one's beliefs! It has so much in common with our own times. Those who make discoveries about the universe then were considered even more heretical than those who are trying now to make something new. What we're experiencing is the battle between dying capitalism and the creators of a new world. Then, like now, the transition from one stage to another was accompanied by wars, political intrigues, terror – everything. Well, time passes, and in the squares where Hus and Bruno were burnt long ago their monuments now stand.[8]

SELECTED WRITINGS:
POLITICS AND THE WOMEN'S QUESTION

The twelve articles put together in this volume by the editors of LeftWord offer a sampling of Kollontai's writings and speeches on a range of themes and issues that preoccupied her at different phases of her political life. The selection, divided into three parts, is arranged chronologically and thematically.

Part 1 contains three articles from 1910-13, dealing with the demands of the socialist women's movement at that historical juncture. The foremost of these demands was the right to vote – non-negotiable in Kollontai's view, but still not accepted by some sections of the international socialist women's movement. In Part 2 – the most substantive of the three sections, which includes a selection of her writings from 1917 to 1927 – Kollontai's primary

---

[8] Ibid., p. 413. Also Farnsworth, 'Bolshevism, the Woman Question, and Aleksandra Kollontai', p. 314.

focus is on how to resolve the women's question *under socialism*, the establishment of which, for her, is a precondition for any meaningful and progressive change in the lives and futures of women. It is also from this perspective that she expounds her views on sexuality and communist morality in relation to the family.

Part 3 contains Kollontai's memoirs. They end in 1926, and include passages she herself had expunged, very likely acting on the directions of the official censors. They provide her reflections on her life and times, and justifications for the choices she made and the decisions she took. Her biographers and later commentators have pointed to the self-censorship that marks Kollontai's memoirs. This could well be true. She may have downplayed certain issues, or even avoided writing about certain events that she knew would get her or others into trouble. However, what is clear is that she did not falsify or invent anything in order to satisfy or please anyone. Therefore, incomplete as they are, the value of her memoirs in the reconstruction of her life and actions remains undiminished.

## PART 1: EARLY DEMANDS OF
## THE SOCIALIST WOMEN'S MOVEMENT

Kollontai's reports on the International Socialist Conferences of Women of 1907 and 1910 – the first two articles in Part 1 – addressed some of the issues that left women's organizations have faced historically. For instance, women workers tended to not join unions of their own volition. Organizing women workers was therefore a pressing duty of proletarian parties, Kollontai argued, and indeed the only way to defeat a ruling class that had 'set one half of the proletariat against the other, shattered its unity, compelled the women to appear as the menacing rivals of their menfolk, sapping the class solidarity of the workers'.

At this stage, however, the focus of her attention was on the demand for equal political rights for women. Kollontai launched a stinging attack on the Social Democratic parties of the time for vacillating on the issue of supporting universal suffrage. She drew attention to a resolution on universal suffrage that had been recently passed at a Social Democratic convention, where the crucial phrase, 'without distinction of sex', was dropped from the text of the resolution. Even some 'consistent and steadfast' supporters of socialism, she noted, did not condemn this opportunist attitude. 'Political equality for proletarian women is part and parcel of the overall class struggle of the proletariat', Kollontai emphasized, and while each country had to shape its tactics in accordance with the specificities of the local situation, to abandon the demand before beginning the fight was unacceptable.

The discussion on voting rights spilled over into the Second Conference of Women, in 1910. Here the delegates were divided over the issue of timing: when should the movement privilege the demand for women's unconditional right to vote? While the left-wing German delegation said that the demand could brook no delay, the English representatives, who worked with the Suffragettes in their country, supported the latter's demand for 'qualified' voting rights for women. However, the left resolution was overwhelmingly adopted by the conference.

The need for a separate and independent platform to formulate and represent the interests of working women within a socialist party may seem obvious enough to Left parties today. However, it was a demand that the early socialist women's movement had to fight hard for. As the two important articles by Kollontai in Part 1 of this volume show, women socialists had to establish the necessity for a proletarian women's movement that was independent yet part of the larger working class movement or party. Kollontai argued the general principles of this relationship of independence based on unity with great reason, urging that a socialist party must consider the specific demands of working women as a 'special objective'. She wrote:

It became clear that the women's proletarian movement was an integral part of the whole movement of the working class. Nonetheless, the specific social and political position of women in contemporary society requires that a particular approach be adopted towards women, and puts before the party a number of special objectives. These objectives, while they form part of the whole working-class movement, while they form part of the common aim, nonetheless affect specifically female interests more closely and are therefore more properly pursued by the *women representatives of the working class themselves.*

A second and related issue that Kollontai resolves in these essays is one that has echoed through the history of working class movements the world over. The defence of the idea of an independent working women's organization had to incorporate a defence against the label of 'bourgeois feminist' thrown at it. In an article written on the occasion of Women's Day in 1908, Kollontai constructed and then deconstructed the argument that an independent working women's organization is a concession to bourgeois feminism. It is worth quoting her polemic at some length.

But, some will say, why this *singling out* of women workers? Why special 'Women's Days', special leaflets for working women, meetings and conferences of working-class women? Is this not, in the final analysis, a concession to the feminists and bourgeois suffragettes?

And the reply:

What is the aim of the feminists? [Kollontai is referring to bourgeois feminists here] Their aim is to achieve the same advantages, the same power, the same rights within capitalist society as those possessed now by their husbands, fathers and brothers.

What is the aim of the women workers? Their aim is to abolish all privileges deriving from birth or wealth. For the woman worker it is a matter of indifference who is the 'master' – a man or a woman.

Together with the whole of her class, she can ease her position as a worker.

Feminists demand equal rights always and everywhere. Women workers reply: we demand rights for every citizen, man and woman, but we are not prepared to forget that we are not only workers and citizens, but also mothers! And as mothers, as women who give birth to the future, we demand special concern for ourselves and our children, special protection from the state and society.

The feminists are striving to acquire political rights. However, here too our paths separate.

For bourgeois women, political rights are simply a means allowing them to make their way more conveniently and more securely in a world founded on the exploitation of the working people. For women workers, political rights are a step along the rocky and difficult path that leads to the desired kingdom of labour.

PART 2: WOMEN AND THE FAMILY IN A WORKERS' STATE

The articles in Part 2 of this volume are from what was perhaps the most politically active phase of Kollontai's life. The October Revolution of 1917 gave her a new vantage point from which to write and speak. She had been made the Commissar for Social Welfare and was a member of the party's Central Committee. Lenin had given the call for 'peace, bread and land', and for Russia's withdrawal from the First World War which was sapping its resources. It was a slogan that resonated with a population facing an acute food crisis and reeling under rising prices. With a workers' and peasants' government in power, expectations were high – even as threats both internal and external loomed. The world was watching. As Commissar, Kollontai had to organize child care, put in place free maternity and infant health care, begin collective kitchens, and reorganize old age facilities.

Kollontai used the women's newspaper *Rabotnitsa* to address the most important issues of the day, in ringing yet fact-intensive prose. Winning and consolidating state power, and introducing progressive and transformative legislation, were important, she argued. But for all this to show results there had to be a cessation of the war into which Russia had been drawn by the previous regime. Calling war 'the most dreadful evil hanging over our heads', Kollontai appealed to all workers – but especially women workers – to 'conduct a tireless, insistent mass struggle to achieve the quickest possible end to world war'. For, as long as war continues, she said, 'we cannot build the new Russia, cannot resolve the problem of bread, of food, cannot halt the rising cost of living'. This was a period when Kollontai worked herself to sickness, but it was also, in her own words, 'the happiest time of my life'. It was a time when the new Soviet government was rushing through new legislations. Finland was given independence and national minorities were awarded the right to self-determination. Private property was nationalized; titles and distinctions of class and sex were abolished; a new civil marriage law was enacted; and a new decree on children gave legal recognition to all children, whether born in or out of marriage. Kollontai participated in the drafting of early Soviet laws that legalized abortion, divorce, birth control and, interestingly, homosexuality.

Despite Kollontai's denunciation of war, she joined the Workers' Opposition group within the government that opposed the Treaty of Brest-Litovsk in 1918. The treaty bought peace for the Soviet Union with Germany, although on very harsh terms. With this major ideological turn, Kollontai's political role in the Bolshevik government began to unravel. The Workers' Opposition was convinced that a socialist revolution was on the anvil in Germany and Austria, and that till that happened, Russia should not capitulate to Germany's onerous terms but fight a guerrilla war against the German army. On the other hand, Lenin was clear that the fledgling Soviet state was not ready to face a German army, and therefore, however harsh the terms of the treaty for Russia, it would give the government and party the breathing space necessary to build its capabilities and attend to the most immediate tasks at hand. At the 10th Congress, the Workers' Opposition was condemned and disbanded, although its leaders continued to hold senior positions in government. Kollontai was dropped from the central committee of the party, and she resigned from her position as Commissar.

Through all this and despite her growing differences with the Bolshevik party, she continued to write in *Rabotnitsa* in its defence. With the end of the First World War, the Soviet government was embroiled in a civil war against its internal enemies who were supported by outside powers. 'This is not war, but the working people rising up in defence of their rights, freedom and very life!', Kollontai wrote in an article, 'What are we fighting for?' (1919). An estimated five to seven million Russians would die in the civil war that lasted two-and-a-half years.[9]

Kollontai, it would appear from her writings of this period, was responding to the urgent public need for knowledge and clarity about current politics and the decisions taken by the Bolshevik government in this intense phase of political change and action. Part 2 of this volume offers a sampling of the range of issues that she privileged for public discussion. In these articles her writing style is declamatory and urgent, and imbued with a sense of exhilaration and optimism at the socialist project under construction. We have her explaining the significance of the first socialist revolution of the world in 'Our Tasks' (1917); presenting the case for implementing the 'dictatorship of the proletariat' by the Bolsheviks in 'Why the Bolsheviks Should Win' (1917); and clarifying the Bolshevik party's call for popular mobilization against the enemies of the Soviet government during the civil war in 'What are we fighting for?' (1919).

On the mobilization of women in support of socialism in general, and the Bolshevik programme in particular, Kollontai

---

[9] Porter, *Alexandra Kollontai*, p. 298.

wrote two major pieces. The first, *On the History of the Movement of Women Workers* (1920), was a tract in which she tried to establish that women's politicization is not a new phenomenon but has a long revolutionary tradition in Russia, which the women's movement could draw inspiration from. In 1921 she wrote *Sexual Relations and Class Struggle*, in which she argued for new forms of partnership between the sexes based on equality and a new socialist morality. Not surprisingly, she was criticized for this by a spectrum of Marxists from both within and outside the party. The more conservative of her critics accused her of succumbing to the demands of bourgeois feminism; others criticized her for an immature sense of political timing. When the very future of the socialist state was at stake, was this the right time to raise issues pertaining to interpersonal relationships? Further, Kollontai's personal conduct at this time only added to the gossip and hostility towards her. She suddenly dropped all pressing work and duties to spend time with Pavel Dybenko, a Red Army officer who was to later become her husband. The fact that he was almost twenty years her junior added to the slurs aimed at her. She was sharply attacked by the Central Committee for her lack of party discipline.

Kollontai believed that the 'sexual crisis', as she called it, needed to be urgently addressed, and what system but socialism could do so? 'Mankind today is living through an acute sexual crisis which is far more unhealthy and harmful for being long and drawn-out', she wrote. Unlike the champions of 'bourgeois individualism' who argue for sexual codes of the past and institutions like the family to be thrown out, socialists 'assure us that sexual problems will only be settled when the basic reorganization of the social and economic structure of society has been tackled'. For Kollontai, however, this was unacceptable. The solution to the crisis had to be found immediately, 'at this very moment'.

Kollontai strongly disagreed with those who argued that sexual relationships belonged to the realm of the personal. The idea of a private world that was distinct from the public was inimical, she believed, to the cause of women's emancipation in a socialist society. 'How can we explain to ourselves the hypocritical way in which *sexual problems* are relegated to the realm of *private matters* that are not worth the effort and attention of the collective?' she asked. Her argument was that if class struggle is the driver of historical change, then, the attempt by the ruling classes to order the relationship between the sexes through their own moral codes is a facet of class struggle. For a socialist party that had captured power, this 'crisis' demanded immediate attention.

What did Kollontai mean by the sexual crisis? The sense of alienation or 'the heavy hand of an unavoidable loneliness of spirit' created by a world of unequal property relationships, sharp class contradictions and individualistic morality, she argued, led men to enter into unprincipled relationships with women, even with the women they chose to marry. The 'crisis' lay in exploitative, loveless and unequal partnerships between the sexes, whether these were inside or outside marriage. There are two factors that underline such relationships, Kollontai said. The first is the idea of 'possessing' the married partner. The second is the belief that the two sexes are unequal in every sphere of activity.

For a marriage to be based on real love, mutual respect and compatibility, there must be a 'radical re-education of our psyche', said Kollontai, and only the socialist state could provide the conditions under which these changes in attitude could take place. The basic notions of bourgeois sexual morality, by which the woman must bear the burden of inequality in personal and public spaces, was already in the process of being 'broken down by the basic principle of the working-class ideology of *comradely solidarity*', Kollontai wrote. But this was not enough. 'Only a change in the economic role of woman, and her independent involvement in production, can and will bring about the weakening of these mistaken and hypocritical ideas.'

And, much like the state which would 'wither away' under communism, the institution of the family too would disappear as the material basis on which it was grounded would cease to exist. But this could only happen with intervention – legislative, educational and agitational – by the workers' state. In Kollontai's words:

> The communist economy does away with the family. In the period of the dictatorship of the proletariat there is a transition to the single production plan and collective social consumption, and the family loses its significance as an economic unit. The external economic functions of the family disappear, and consumption ceases to be organized on an individual family basis. A network of social kitchens and canteens is established, and the making, mending and washing of clothes and other aspects of housework are integrated into the national economy. In the period of the dictatorship of the proletariat, the family economic unit should be recognized as being, from the point of view of the national economy, not only useless but also harmful. The family economic unit involves (a) the uneconomic expenditure of products and fuel on the part of small domestic economies, and (b) unproductive labour, especially by women in the home – and is therefore in conflict with the interest of the workers' republic in a single economic plan and the expedient use of the labour force (including women).

Women, once given productive value independent of the family, become truly free. The workers' collective would also take full responsibility for the care of children, and their 'physical and spiritual education', she predicted, thus creating a new relationship between parents and children.

Kollontai then took the argument a step further. A stage will come, she said, when the state does not have to recognize a married couple as a legal unit separate from the workers' collective: it only recognizes its obligation to guarantee the well-being of the woman during maternity, and of the child until it becomes an adult. Once these arrangements are in place and accepted, the decrees on marriage that the workers' republic would have issued when it first assumed office would become 'survivals of the past', and, in Kollontai's view, would logically be discarded. After all, she argued, an institution like the family with its self-centred interests would only 'contradict the interests of the collective and weaken its bond'.

It was only when the workers' collective entered this stage that the 'sexual crisis' would be resolved. 'In the period of the dictatorship of the proletariat,' Kollontai said, 'communist morality – and not the law – regulates sexual relationships in the interest of the workers' collective and of future generations.' No longer would the sexual act be morally judged; instead it would become something as 'natural as the other needs of a healthy organism such as hunger and thirst'. It was this comment that led her most trenchant critics to denounce what came to be known as the 'glass of water' theory of sexuality.

In the two articles 'Sexual Relations and the Class Struggle' (1921) and 'Theses on Communist Morality in the Sphere of Marital Relations' (1921), Kollontai was taking the long view. She believed that the dictatorship of the proletariat – a strategy to preserve and strengthen the workers' state – should be extended to the realm of the family and interpersonal relationships, an area rife with false consciousness. Only a workers' state could liberate the working class and other exploited sections from this. Indeed sensitivity was called for, and the state should not act as if it were dealing with class enemies, she said. Rather, a well-thought-out intervention that had both legislative and educational components was required to achieve this. 'The task of proletarian ideology is not to drive Eros from social life, but to rearm him according to the new social formation, and to transform sexual relationships in the spirit of the great new psychological force of comradely solidarity,' she wrote in 1923, in an article published in *Young Guard* titled 'Make way for winged Eros'.[10]

The publication of this and other similar pieces on the subject

---

[10] Porter, *Alexandra Kollontai*, p. 385.

drew sustained and virulent attacks from critics.[11] One of her former colleagues at the Zhenotdel, Paulina Vinogradskaya, in an article titled 'Questions of Sex, Morality and Everyday Life', attacked Kollontai's views as anti-Marxist and typical of petit-bourgeois intellectuals who enjoyed the comforts of living abroad while offering prescriptions for regulating the personal lives of people back home. 'But then Comrade Kollontai was always wont to swim in a sea of banal phrases, diluted with a sickly sentimentality and adorned with rhetorical curl-papers', wrote Vinogradskaya. She reminded readers of Kollontai's disregard for party discipline, alleging that she 'put the sexual struggle over class struggle'. Kollontai's use of the term 'multifaceted love' only meant multiple relationships and casual sex, Vinogradskaya alleged.

A series of unsigned articles that *Pravda* ran around the same time cruelly parodied Kollontai's views. Nadhezda Krupskaya and Natalya Sedova, Trotsky's wife, also criticized Kollontai's interpretation of feminism. In addition to all this, Kollontai was repeatedly questioned by the Control Commission about her former political links with the Workers' Opposition. She finally asked for and was granted an interview with Stalin, to whom she complained about being harassed and interrogated for ideas she had once held but long abandoned. The interrogations stopped, and Kollontai returned to Oslo where she was posted as the Soviet ambassador.

PART 3: MEMOIRS

It was therefore an utterly misunderstood and misrepresented Kollontai who narrated her personal story in a short autobiography – published in 1926 and reprinted in Part 3 of this volume. Her tone here is defensive as she earnestly outlines the impulses and ideals that made her the woman and communist she chose to be. The

[11] Ibid., pp. 385-86.

autobiography, published when she was in Norway, was written in response to the harsh and bruising takedown she had received at the hands of critics for her views on marriage and sexuality, referred to earlier. Thoroughly discredited in the Russian press, she chose to tell her own story. The autobiography is therefore pervaded with the sense of injustice Kollontai felt as a woman whose successes were won through struggle and suffering in an essentially male-dominated world.

A second important aspect of her autobiography relates to censorship. Kollontai expunged several sentences and passages in the draft manuscript. Wherever she had taken personal credit for some action, the attribution was changed from I to 'we', or sometimes 'the Soviet state'. Secondly, all passages in which she justified her conduct and personal choices with respect to her romantic life were dropped, as were replies to critics that contained deprecating comments on the backwardness of Russian society's outlook, especially towards women. Finally, descriptions and reconstructions of political events that contained negative references to the party, or individuals in the party, were either toned down or dropped. Nevertheless, even with all the cuts and rewriting, the book retains a defiant if somewhat breathless tone.

In response to those who slandered her personally Kollontai had this to say:

I have succeeded in structuring my intimate life according to my own standards and I make no secret of my love experiences any more than does a man. Above all, however, I never let my feelings, the joy or pain of love take the first place in my life inasmuch as creativity, activity, struggle always occupied the foreground.

She saw her life as an example to other women.

What is of a wholly special significance here is that a woman, like myself, who has settled scores with the double standard and who has never concealed it, was accepted into a caste which to this very day staunchly upholds tradition and pseudo-morality. Thus the example of my life can also serve to dispel the old goblin of the double standard also from the lives of other women. And this is a most crucial point of my own existence, which has a certain social-psychological worth and contributes to the liberation struggle of working women. . . . I had above all set myself the task of winning over women workers in Russia to socialism.

Thus, Kollontai makes the plea again and again in her autobiography that she be judged for the work she has done and not for her personal life-choices, or the fact that she is a woman. She writes of the hard work she put into every task she undertook and of her firm commitment to the ideals of socialism. She attributes her successes and the positions she has held to the women's movement, and sees them as a 'symbol of the fact that woman, after all, is already on the march to general recognition'. It was 'the drawing of millions of women into productive work, which was swiftly effected especially during the war . . . which thrust into the realm of possibility the fact that a woman could be advanced to the highest political and diplomatic positions'.

It is unfortunate that the task of highlighting her achievements and defending her contributions – to the revolutionary cause, and to the cause of women in Russia and the rest of the world – was left to Kollontai herself, at least in her lifetime. Although she received high recognition in her home country, which included a nomination to the Nobel Peace Prize, it is apparent that she did not achieve popular national status in the country she loved and worked for so selflessly. Kollontai was not to become an icon or even a role model for the women's movement, nor were her contributions to Soviet diplomacy during the critical years between 1923 and 1945 sufficiently acknowledged.

Recognition did come, but only partially and not in her own country, in the decades following her death. Biographies on

Kollontai appeared in the English-speaking world, and her life and writings became topics for theoretical discussion in feminist literature, including within that section of the feminist movement whose forebears she so resolutely opposed in her lifetime. Within Left and working class movements, too, there is little meaningful understanding of her ideas and contributions, and their contemporary relevance. That is surely a loss, for Kollontai's life is undoubtedly an inspiring one. The storehouse of views reflecting her socialist outlook, and her practical experiences that contributed to the success of the socialist revolution in Russia are part of the socialist legacy. In hindsight, some of these views were perhaps misconceived, some even wrong. An individual's contributions rarely come packed in a parcel of political perfection. But Kollontai was a participant in world history at a crucial turning point, and what better time to recover her forgotten legacy than now, when the 100th anniversary of that epochal event is being celebrated?

# PART 1

# INTERNATIONAL

# WOMEN'S DAY

## THE FIRST INTERNATIONAL CONFERENCE
## OF SOCIALIST WOMEN
Stuttgart, 1907

A new danger is threatening the domination of the bourgeoisie – women workers are resolutely adopting the path of international class organization. The downtrodden, submissive slaves humbly bowing before the omnipotence of the modern Moloch of capital are, under the reviving influence of socialist doctrine, lifting their heads and raising their voices in defence of their interests as women and their common class interests.

While the 'poison of socialist doctrine' had infected only one half of the working class, while opposition was concentrated exclusively in the male section of the proletariat, the capitalists could breathe freely; they still had in their power an inexhaustible supply of compliant workers always ready obediently and selflessly to enrich by their labour the happy owners of the instruments of production. With unconscious calculation the bourgeoisie availed itself of the advantage offered by this state of affairs: it set one half of the proletariat against the other, shattered its unity, compelled the women to appear as the menacing rivals of their menfolk, sapping the class solidarity of the workers. With malicious smugness it countered the resistance of united proletarians with the indifference of the unconscious female elements, and the more ignorant and dispersed the women remained, the more unsuccessful was the struggle waged by the organized elements of the working class.

However, the class consciousness of the women workers, once aroused, was sufficient to compel them to grasp the hand of friendship held out to them by their male worker comrades and adopt the path of open and stubborn resistance. The involvement of proletarian women in the common class struggle, and their growing solidarity have shaken the usual self-confidence of the bourgeoisie and spread alarm in place of its previous tranquility: the increasing organization of the female proletariat removes the last defenceless victim of capitalist exploitation. The ground is disappearing from beneath the feet of the bourgeoisie, and the light of the approaching social revolution glows ever more brightly.

Is it therefore surprising that the bourgeoisie is doubly hostile to any sign of protest among women workers, and to any attempt on their part to defend their needs and interests as women and their common class interests and needs? Even in the most democratic and advanced countries everything possible is done to make it difficult for women to defend their labour interests. To grant the woman worker the same rights as the man would be to put in the hands of the working class a new and dangerous weapon, to double the active army of the militant opponent; the bourgeoisie is too intelligent to agree to such a dangerous experiment.

The whole bourgeois world listened with unconcealed animosity to the solemn and harmonious notes that rang out from Stuttgart in 1907, during the International Socialist Congress.[1] But most of all it was angered by the bold voices of the female proletariat. However radical were the speeches pronounced by the men, whatever 'mad' resolutions they might adopt, the bourgeoisie always consoled itself with the thought that it still had one tested method at its disposal: break the resistance of the 'hotheads' by replacing them with submissive female workers. And now a new surprise: from all over the world women representatives of the working class are gathering in order to forge by their united efforts a new weapon

---

[1] This is a reference to the Seventh International Congress of the Second International, held in Stuttgart on 18-24 August, 1907. The Congress was attended by delegates from 25 countries, including Argentina, Austria, Belgium, Bulgaria, Denmark, England, Germany, Italy, Norway, Poland, Russia and the USA – 886 delegates in all. The Bolshevik delegation was led by Lenin, who did a great deal of work to consolidate the left-wing forces of international Social-Democracy. The Congress adopted a resolution committing socialists to oppose the approaching war.

with which to fight the world hostile to the proletariat.[2] The daring of women has exceeded all expectations: yesterday's silent slave is now a courageous fighter for the liberation of the working class. Could one imagine a more vexatious spectacle! Spiteful ridicule rained down upon the heads of the women representatives of the working class, ridicule that failed to conceal the genuine anxiety of the bourgeoisie.

The gentlemen of capital and property do now indeed have something to ponder over, something to be depressed about: new successes are being achieved in the organization of the working class. And if, until only recently, the bourgeoisie could draw comfort from the lack of unity in the female section of the proletariat, now, after the Stuttgart Conference, it has lost even this sweet solace.

On the basis of facts and figures these women representatives described the growing awareness of the female proletariat and its organizational successes, particularly in recent years. England has the largest number of organized women workers: 150,000 are members of trade unions; 30,000 are politically organized in 'independent workers' parties and women workers are also members of the Social-Democratic Federation.[3] In Austria trade union organizations include 42,000 women among their members. In Germany the number of women who are trade union members is also impressive – 120,000; despite all the police harassment, 10,500 women workers have joined the Social-Democratic Party, and the distribution figure for the women workers' magazine *Die Gleichheit*

---

[2] In 1907, just before the opening of the International Socialist Congress in Stuttgart, the First International Conference of Socialist Women was held, attended by 58 women delegates from 14 countries. The main aim of the conference was to formulate one united tactic for all the Socialist parties in the campaign to win voting rights for women workers as part of universal and equal voting rights for both sexes.

[3] *The Social-Democratic Federation* – founded in England in 1884, declared itself a socialist organization, but did not recognize Marxism. It had no contact with the workers and was extremely sectarian in nature. In 1907 it was renamed the Social-Democratic Party.

(Equality) is 70,000 copies.[4] In Finland the Social-Democratic movement has 18,600 women. In Belgium 14,000 women workers are trade union members. In Hungary 15,000 women workers are in trade union organizations, etc.

The growing organization of women workers and the specific social objectives which it is mainly their task to carry through led to an awareness of the need for greater solidarity and closer contact among the organized women workers of the world.

The first women's international conference in Stuttgart set itself two objectives: (1) to elaborate the basis for more uniform activity on the part of the socialist movement (in various countries) in the struggle to win voting rights for women workers; (2) to establish permanent and correct relations between women's organizations throughout the world.

The main question discussed at the conference was, without any doubt, the question of voting rights for women workers. Put forward for discussion by the conference and introduced into the Social-Democratic congress as a special resolution, this question is designed to meet the growing need within the female proletariat to define the future tactics of international Social-Democracy in the struggle for political rights for women workers, and to transfer this principle from the sphere of theoretical recognition to that of practical activity. With the growth of its class consciousness and organization, the female proletariat was brought by its basic material needs to an acute awareness of its lack of political rights, and learned to see in those rights not only a 'policy principle' but also an urgent and immediate need.

Over recent years, the working class, in one country after the other, has faced the question of achieving universal suffrage. It might have seemed that the four-part election formula advanced by the Social-Democrats and supplemented with a fifth section

[4] *Die Gleichheit* (Equality) – a Social-Democratic bimonthly magazine issued by the women's proletarian movement in Germany. It was published from 1890 to 1925, and was edited by Clara Zetkin from 1892 to 1917.

specifying 'without distinction of sex', would have left no room for doubts and hesitations regarding the way the party would act in such circumstances. However, it turned out otherwise. When it came to the defence of the fifth section, not only male Social-Democrats, but even the women revealed their fundamental instability, their vacillation, and by their compromising attitude to this issue, so important to the working class, demonstrated that this fundamental principle has not yet become an integral part of Social-Democracy.

One after the other women from Belgium, Austria, Sweden, accepted the removal from the agenda of the demand for political rights for women workers and gave their support to an emasculated, abbreviated compromise formula for electoral reform. However, most characteristic of all was the fact that this opportunist policy was not condemned by consistent and steadfast supporters of socialism but, on the contrary, won their sympathy and approval and was even presented to proletarian women in other countries as a model. The working women themselves cannot be blamed for this compromise tactic – it is typical of less aware and less disciplined party elements but the other, the male section of the proletariat, whose spirit and consciousness has been tempered in battle, should not have allowed itself to be drawn along the path of practical opportunism.

There are democratic principles which, for the sake of its own interests, the working class must not sacrifice: there are slogans which the proletariat cannot change without damaging itself, even though the change is made in order to achieve the maximum results at any given moment.

If, in some politically backward country, the working class had had the opportunity to attain universal, equal, secret but indirect rather than direct voting rights, the position of the Social-Democrats in such a situation would have been obvious: despite the risk of stalling a reform that was otherwise certain to be adopted, the workers' party would fight to the last moment for the full formula. . . . Perhaps the indirect electoral system would be adopted despite the opposition of the Social-Democrats, and no doubt they would have to reconcile themselves to this fact, but their attitude to it would be perfectly clear: they could view it only as a defeat.

The situation is different as regards the issue of voting rights for women workers. The demand 'without distinction of sex' has not yet become an integral part of the practice of proletarian struggle: awareness of the importance of full and equal political rights for women workers in the name of the interests of the whole class has not yet had time to take firm root. It must not be forgotten that women began to work outside the home only comparatively recently, and have only recently begun to play a role in the proletarian movement. The ideological survivals of the bourgeois-capitalist world affect the purity and clarity of proletarian class consciousness in regard to women, and blur the distinct outlines of a principle that would appear to be indisputable in the eyes of the proletariat, namely the principle of equality of civil rights for all the members of the world proletarian family.

The vacillating tactic of the party in the struggle for women's voting rights obliged the Social-Democrats to devote particular attention to this issue at the congress. The adoption of a resolution which would clearly and precisely express the willingness of the working class to fight for voting rights for women workers with the same unswerving determination with which Social-Democracy pursues all its principles – this was the slogan of the women's socialist conference, a slogan dictated by the interests of women workers. Such a resolution appeared all the more desirable in that it was fully in accord with the spirit of Social-Democracy. . . .

The resolution on voting rights for women put forward at the women's conference and then introduced at the socialist congress was advanced with a view to demanding the clear and precise recognition of the fifth section of the election formula ('without distinction of sex') as being of equal importance with the other four.

However, the resolution met with opposition. Two trends appeared within the women's socialist movement: one orthodox, the other opportunist in the spirit of unconscious feminism. The first trend was represented by the women Social-Democrats from Germany, the second by those from Austria and some from England.

The resolution put forward by the German delegates had two objectives: in demanding that the socialist parties recognize the full extent of the importance of a practical struggle to secure the political equality of women, the resolution was also intended to draw a distinct line between bourgeois feminism and the women's proletarian movement. This struck the English socialists at their most vulnerable point. It is a well-known fact that many of them work hand-in-glove with bourgeois champions of women's rights, and in the heat of a sometimes selfless struggle in defence of women's interests, they lose sight of class distinctions.

The struggle to achieve political equality for *proletarian women* is part and parcel of the overall class struggle of the proletariat; when it becomes an independent militant aim in itself it eclipses the class objectives of women workers. The inventive bourgeoisie, who love to hide their real desires behind a screen of splendid-sounding slogans, put the world of women and its objectives in opposition to the class cause of women workers. However, as soon as the women's cause is put above the proletarian cause, as soon as women workers allow themselves to be seduced by fine-sounding phrases about the community of women's interests regardless of class divisions, they lose their living link with their own class cause and thus betray their own particular interests. Bourgeois women, according to their own assertion, are generously demanding rights for 'all women', whereas women workers are only fighting for their class interests. However, in practice the situation is precisely the reverse: in winning political rights for themselves, women workers are also opening up the way to the voting booth for women of other classes. In resolutely and consistently defending the interests of the women of its own class, Social-Democracy is putting into practice the principles of the fullest form of democracy and promoting the success of the women's cause as a whole.

Bourgeois hypocrisy also affected the English supporters of women's political equality. English women workers are prepared to support *limited, qualified* electoral rights for women – an unforgivable and despicable betrayal of the proletarian cause. The representatives of the Independent Labour Party and the Fabian Society did not hesitate to defend this clearly treacherous position before the whole socialist world, and only the Social-Democratic Federation, together with the proletariat of other countries, condemned such a solution to the problem and demanded electoral rights for all citizens who had reached majority, regardless of sex.[5]

This disagreement yet again clearly demonstrated the importance for the socialists of working out a clearly defined tactical position on the question of achieving political equality for women workers. However, such a clearly defined formulation of the question was precisely what the English wanted least. . . . Together with the Austrian delegates they demanded that each party be given the right to settle this question independently in accord with the circumstances then obtaining; they declared a single model of action compulsory for each country to be completely unnecessary. The resolution put forward by the German Social-Democrats obliged the English to do some painful thinking. It faced them

[5] *The Independent Labour Party* – founded in England in 1893. Its aims were to secure the election of workers to Parliament in order to pursue its own independent policies, to campaign for the nationalization of land and the means of production, and also to work within the trade unions. It soon lost its militant spirit under the influence of bourgeois fellow-travellers, and its leadership became opportunist. *The Fabian Society* – founded in England in 1884 by representatives of the bourgeois intelligentsia. The Fabians rejected class struggle, and proposed a programme of state or municipal 'socialism', hoping to transform capitalist society into a socialist society by means of gradual reform.

with a question: are they defending the interests of their class as a whole in its difficult struggle to survive, passing through great trials today in the expectation of equally great triumphs in the future, or are they merely fighting for new privileges for those women who neither sow nor reap, but who gather into the barns?

The Austrian delegates represented the opposite extreme. Furious opponents of feminism, they were not, of course, prepared to work together with bourgeois feminists in the defence of rights for 'all women'. However, despite their sworn hostility towards feminism and its tactic of adaptation, Austrian women socialists fell into the same error as the English. In defending at the conference the position they had adopted during the recent struggle in Austria to achieve universal suffrage, they attempted to show that, in certain political conditions, it is permissible to put aside the interests of one section of the proletariat – in this case women workers – in order to achieve practical advantages for another section. Instead of a categorical demand that the principle of political equality for proletarian women be recognized on the same footing with all other democratic demands by the proletariat, the Austrians introduced into the resolution by means of an amendment a poorly-defined wish that the *moment* and the *very method of struggle* for electoral rights for women be determined by each country at its own discretion. . . .

Every time the question of party tactics becomes a matter of urgency for Social-Democracy, it has to return to the tested method of solving this question: it must once more carefully and precisely determine to what extent a given demand, a given principle is essential in order to achieve the ultimate objective of the working class. If this principle is indeed of considerable importance for the ultimate objective being pursued by the workers, then there cannot be, must not be, any room for compromise in policy even if such a compromise promises to bring immediate benefit. Indeed, what would become of the class objectives of the proletariat if Social-Democracy put away its basic policy principles every time it hoped it might thereby acquire some 'practical advantage'? And what would then distinguish its policy principles from hypocritical bourgeois diplomacy?

The principle of political equality for women is beyond dispute. Social-Democracy long ago proclaimed in theory the importance of extending voting rights to women workers. However, the tactic of 'concessions', the tactic of 'step by step' is now seeking another solution to this problem also. In place of the usual principled determination and steadfastness of Social-Democracy, it proposes 'compliance' and 'moderation'. Fortunately the proletariat is only too well aware that its 'modesty' has never reaped any reward. The tractability and compliance of the proletariat are, in the eyes of its enemy, proof positive of its 'impotence', and the more moderate, the more 'reasonable' are its demands, the more miserly are the concessions granted to it. The victory of one of the two warring sides is decided not by the compliance of one of them, but by the 'actual balance of forces'. The proletariat presses its demands waging a resolute and consistent struggle to achieve them, but it can only achieve that which corresponds to its actual influence and importance at any given moment. The more resolute is Social-Democracy's adherence to its basic principles, the further removed its tactic from concessions decided upon beforehand, the more closely will the results of its struggle correspond to the actual balance of power and forces between the warring sides.

All of the above constitutes a 'well-worn truth', but a truth that has to be repeated every time a proposed compromise tactic postpones a new victory by the proletariat and threatens to damage one of the basic tenets of Social-Democracy. If the amendment introduced by the Austrian delegates were accepted, such damage would be unavoidable. With their precautionary 'compliance' the Austrian delegates would not only postpone the extension of voting rights to proletarian women but also, and more importantly, violate one of the basic principles of socialism: preserving the unity of the working class as the major guarantee of success in the proletarian struggle.

'Naturally,' said Clara Zetkin, addressing the commission on women's voting rights at the congress, 'we are not so politically uneducated as to demand that the socialist parties of every country, in every struggle for electoral reform and in all circumstances, make the demand for voting rights for women the cornerstone, the deciding factor in their struggle.' That will depend on the level of historical development in individual countries. We are criticizing the tactic of 'abandoning in advance, without a struggle, the demand for voting rights for women. . . .'

This precise and consistent class policy was also defended by German Social-Democrats: Luise Zietz, Emma Ihrer, Ottilie Baader, Hilja Pärssinen, woman deputy to the Finnish Seim, Csozi from Hungary, representatives from Russia, Shaw from England and others. Those who supported this view demanded that the international congress confirm the proposition that the struggle for voting rights for women workers is not separate from the class struggle, and that any concession in this area, any deviation from principle, is a compromise that damages the whole cause of the working class.

The defenders of the opportunist tactic came mainly from among the Austrian delegates, and they received a measure of support from Viktor Adler. Lily Braun was also on their side. However, this trend did not meet support at the conference. All the arguments advanced by the Austrians to the effect that the 'obstinacy' of the Social-Democrats only served to make political gains by the proletariat more difficult to achieve, all the arguments of the representatives of Catholic countries – Belgium and France – that the influence of clericalism would allegedly increase with the involvement of women in politics and would lead to a regrouping of parliamentary representation to the disadvantage of the working class, paled before the indisputable fact that the most impoverished, exploited section of the proletariat women workers are still deprived of the possibility of opposing the violation of their rights. It is to these pariahs of contemporary society, these pale, worn slaves of capitalism, that their comrades in misery, their comrades in the struggle for a brighter future, preach resignation, patience and self-denial – the clichéd, pharisaical virtues of the bourgeoisie! . . .

The mood of the conference was not favourable to such trends. In contrast to the usual 'respectful obedience' of women, the conference was marked by a lively, bracing atmosphere quite distinct from the somewhat dry, businesslike air of the socialist congress itself. The massive organizational structure of the congress, the presence of almost 900 delegates and the need to observe a whole series of formalities cooled the enthusiasm of the representatives of the socialist world, and only now and again was this enthusiasm able to break through to the surface and affect all those taking part. Here at the congress the most experienced 'masters of the spoken word', skilled in all the finer points of parliamentary battle, crossed verbal swords, but perhaps for this very reason many of them sounded excessively 'cautious'. . . .

At the women's conference, on the other hand, the living pulse of bold faith and confidence beat without ceasing and one could sense that courageous rejection of and revulsion towards compromise decisions which are characteristic of organizations that are still young and have not yet become set in fixed forms. The majority of the representatives of proletarian women could not but realize what tragic consequences would follow upon the adoption of the Austrian amendment. . . .

By a majority of 47 votes to 11, the women's socialist conference adopted the resolution put forward by the German delegation and placed it before the socialist congress.

The living spirit of proletarian self-consciousness compelled the representatives of the workers to support this resolution and confirm the principle of the common interests of both sexes, their solidarity in the struggle for political rights for the whole of the working class. This is without doubt a major event in the 'history of the workers' movement', demonstrating yet again to the bourgeois world that, despite repeated assertions about the 'death of Marxism', the true spirit of scientific socialism is still alive and is continually inspiring the many millions who make up international Social-Democracy.

The question of the formation of an international women's socialist secretariat was second on the conference agenda. The German Social-Democrats introduced a proposal to establish closer contacts among representatives of the working class from different countries and to set up for this purpose a secretariat which would gather information on the women's proletarian movement everywhere. Although this question was purely organizational, it provoked a lively exchange of opinions, and once more revealed two heterogeneous trends within the women's section of Social-Democracy.

The proposal to form an independent women's international secretariat was put forward by the German delegates, and the Austrian delegates once again introduced an amendment. Having declared themselves opposed to separating proletarian women in any way whatsoever, they considered it unnecessary to form a separate secretariat to ensure international communication among women workers. In their opinion, comrades abroad could be kept informed on the state of the women's proletarian movement in each country by empowering a member of the party in each country to send reports on the position of women workers' organizations and on successes achieved by the movement to the central socialist organs of the other countries. This amendment vividly illustrates the constant fear on the part of the Austrians of discrediting themselves by a too clearly-marked defence of 'women's interests' which might earn them the label 'feminists'. . . .

The German Social-Democrats, on the contrary, defended the

idea that an independent grouping of *proletarian* women *within the party* has clear organizational advantages. Such an organization would make it possible to concentrate the attention of the party on the specific needs and requirements of women workers, and would also make it easier to rally around the party the generally less aware female members of the proletarian class.

The involvement of women workers in the party is necessitated by practical and urgent considerations. Up till now women workers remain the most deprived section of the proletarian family, they are still oppressed everywhere by 'special laws', and even in countries which have broad democratic representation women alone remain *without rights.*

With every year that passes, involvement in the political life of their country is becoming an increasingly urgent issue for the women of the working class. However, among the broad masses of the male proletariat the urgency of this demand is not as yet sufficiently recognized.

In order to defend this demand, in order to inculcate in their comrades the proper attitude to the question of equal rights for women workers in every sphere and draw them into the struggle to attain in practice equal civil rights for women, women have only one course – to unite their forces around the party. Women workers must set up a women's secretariat, a commission, a bureau within the party, not in order to wage a separate battle for political rights and defend their own interests by themselves but in order to exert pressure on the party *from within,* in order to compel their comrades to wage their struggle in the interests of the female proletariat as well.

Thus greater party concern about the specific requirements of women workers will increase the popularity of the party among the less class-conscious female population, stimulating the flow of new forces into the army of the fighting proletariat, while the unification of women workers within the party will allow this homogeneous core, motivated by the same requirements, to defend its specific requirements and needs more resolutely within the party too. It was not only police obstacles that led in Germany to special, separate propaganda work among women: this method of work is gradually being adopted in other countries living under freer political regimes.

The need to unite women's forces within the party is, of course, felt with particular force in countries where it is only the women who remain without political rights. In those cases where the question of the struggle for the further democratization of voting rights is to the fore, the core of class-conscious women workers can only strive to ensure a more steadfast attitude in the party towards the question of achieving voting rights for women also. . . .

The position of proletarian women in contemporary society, and the specific needs which they experience in the field of social relations, create a practical basis for conducting special work among the female proletariat. However, such a grouping of proletarian women within the party (the setting up of commissions, bureaus, sections, etc.) has, of course, nothing in common with feminism. Whereas the feminists are struggling to extend to the women of the bourgeois classes those privileges which were hitherto enjoyed only by the men, women workers are pursuing a solely proletarian, common class objective.

At the women's international conference, the victory went to the left, that is, to that section which suggested the creation of an independent international secretariat. The editorial board of *Die Gleichheit* (Equality) has been elected as the central organ of the international movement of socialist women until the next international congress. There can be no doubt that both this purely organizational decision and also the congress resolution on tactics, a resolution which determines the attitude of Social-Democracy to the question of votes for women, will have a beneficial effect upon the further development of the Social-Democratic movement among women workers, and will promote the more rapid growth of the organized army of the female proletariat.

Only if they are firmly united amongst themselves and, at the same time, one with their class party in the common class struggle, can women workers cease to appear as a brake on the proletarian movement and march confidently forward, arm in arm with their male worker comrades to the noble and cherished proletarian aim – towards a new, better and brighter future.

# THE SECOND INTERNATIONAL WOMEN'S CONFERENCE
Copenhagen, 1910

When the First International Conference of Socialist Women was held in Stuttgart in 1907 on the initiative of the German socialists, the women's socialist movement was still in its infancy everywhere except Germany. Its shape was still hazy and unclear, and the conference itself was convened not so much to review what had been already achieved as to give its 'blessing' to the movement and stimulate its further development. Stuttgart was merely a *symptom* of the awakening of broad masses of working-class women, but a symptom nonetheless significant, promising and pregnant with consequences. . . .

Three years have passed. During this short period of time the women's proletarian movement has succeeded not only in increasing its numbers, but also in becoming a social force which cannot be ignored in the process of the class struggle. Particularly rapid has been the success achieved by Germany in the organization of the female proletariat: according to the data presented at the conference in Stuttgart, that is, in 1907 the Social-Democratic Party had only some 10,000 women members; by 1910 it already had more than 82,000, and the central socialist organ for women workers *Die Gleichheit* (Equality) had a circulation of 80,000. Similar giant strides have been taken by Austria in the organization of working-class women: in 1909 the party had only 7,000 women members; in 1910 it had more than 14,000, the trade union movement had around 44,000 women members and the women workers' newspaper had a circulation of 20,000. Finland, though small in population, was also not left behind. Here women (more than 16,000) accounted for some 31 per cent of the membership of the workers' party. England can boast of more than 200,000 women trade union members. Everywhere – in Denmark, Sweden, Norway, Switzerland, Holland, Italy, the United States – the women of the working class are awakening, attempting to create a women's socialist movement and direct it along the path boldly marked out by the energetic efforts of German women socialists.

According to the calculations made by the Swiss delegation, the numerical relationship between the male and female sections of the organized working class in various countries is as follows:

Finland: For every 1 organized woman worker there are 6 organized male workers.

Denmark: For every 1 organized woman worker there are 8 organized male workers.

Austria: For every 1 organized woman worker there are 10 organized male workers.

England: For every 1 organized woman worker there are 11 organized male workers.

Italy: For every 1 organized woman worker there are 12 organized male workers.

Sweden & Norway: For every 1 organized woman worker there are 13 organized male workers.

Germany: For every 1 organized woman worker there are 14 organized male workers.

Switzerland: For every 1 organized woman worker there are 18 organized male workers.

[*Statistical Report* to the Second International Conference of Socialist Women, 1910, p. 26.]

Of course, if these figures are compared with the number of women workers on the labour market and the growing number of women earning their own living in every country, the scale of female participation in the workers movement appears very modest even insignificant. However, in order to assess the importance of the women's socialist movement accurately, two things must be remembered: firstly, its short history – 15-20 years ago it had never been heard of; secondly, the *prospects* opening up before it. The question of the further democratization of the electoral system, which is now posing itself in one form or another in England and the United States, in the federal states of Germany and the Scandinavian countries, must have and will have its inevitable effect upon the further development and success of the women's proletarian movement. The women's proletarian movement has ceased to be merely a luxury and become a daily practical necessity. . . .

The growth of the women's proletarian movement over the last three years was noticeable at the opening of the Copenhagen Conference. In Stuttgart the delegates numbered 52, in Copenhagen they already numbered around 100 and represented 17 countries. This time only the French and the Belgians were absent. Socialist parties and trade unions were represented, together with clubs, societies, and unions of women workers adopting a class position.

The conference agenda included, in addition to the organizational question of establishing closer links between organized socialist women from different countries, two major issues: (1) ways and means of achieving in practice universal suffrage for women, and (2) social security and protection for mother and child. Despite these seemingly specifically female topics, the conference in Copenhagen was free of that sickly-sweet 'feminine flavour' which provokes such irrepressible boredom in the practical politician who is used to the 'cut and thrust' of real political battle. . . . The questions discussed at the conference were examined not only from the point of view of the common tasks of proletarian class policy, but were also, and inevitably, supplemented with more general demands. The fate of Finland, a country with an extremely democratic system of popular representation, the question of war, peace and the fight against militarism, the struggle against domestic manufacture and night work, compelled those taking part in the congress to move beyond the narrow framework of feminine issues and, having become more familiar with wide-ranging, urgent issues, to join in the active struggle being waged by the many millions who compose the army of the organized working class.

However, while one cannot object to the position adopted by the conference on the issues it debated, and while, indeed, one can note with satisfaction that the 'women's worker army' is marching side by side with the whole proletarian movement, it must be stated that, in terms of the formal conduct of its conferences, the women representatives of international socialism still have something to learn from their male colleagues. The lack of familiarity with 'parliamentary practice' led to a number of omissions, which gave rise to misunderstanding and dissatisfaction: certain resolutions were not only not put to the vote, but were not even debated; debates were bunched together, questions were removed from the agenda on the decision of a questionable majority, etc. All of these errors could have been avoided with greater experience. . . .

The main topic discussed at the conference was, of course, that of voting rights. The conflict between the left wing of the women's international, led by the German delegation, and the representatives of those English workers' organizations who work together with the suffragettes and thus support the slogan of *qualified* electoral rights, was inevitable. The English produced as their 'trump card' the venerable and well-known socialist and champion of the women's cause, Charlotte Despard, whose personal attractiveness, noble bearing, grey hair and skillful, impressive speech was intended to win sympathy and soften the severity of the left-wing judgement. A 'furious battle' was expected. However, although the discussion was lively, the expected 'battle' did not take place: from the very beginning it was clear that the overwhelming majority at the conference supported the 'left', and that the English were fighting for a lost cause. . . . The ease with which victory over the 'right' was won is explained in part by the fact that, with the exception of Despard, they did not have one good orator on their side. The English defence lacked spirit and imagination, their arguments in defence of their tactic were naive, almost 'genteel' – the 'harmony' of women's interests, complaints against the 'harshness' of class politics, against social injustice, which also affected the bourgeois woman. . . .

The conference, sharply criticizing cooperation between English socialists and the bourgeois suffragettes, adopted a resolution which, however, failed to stress this aspect sufficiently. 'The women's socialist movement in every country rejects qualified electoral rights,' runs the resolution, as a falsification and as an insult to the very principle of political equality for women. The movement is fighting for the only viable and concrete expression of this principle: universal suffrage for all women who have reached their majority, without qualifications of property, tax, education or any other kind which hinder members of the working class from availing themselves of their civil rights. The women's socialist movement wages its struggle not together with the women's bourgeois movement, but in close cooperation with socialist parties, who are defending electoral rights for women as one of the basic and, in practice, one of the most essential demands in the call for the full democratization of the electoral system. The conciliatory note sounded by the Austrian delegate, Adelheid Popp, in a speech intended to soften the harshness of this judgement found no support, and the resolution was passed by an overwhelming majority, with ten votes against.

On the issue of maternity insurance and protection, no serious differences emerged, and it was only a formal oversight on the part of the presidium that caused conflict with part of the English delegation, which then left the conference hall. The resolution introduced by the German delegation on this issue repeated in essence the basic demands of the Social-Democrats, as developed and supplemented at the women's conference in Mannheim: the demand for an 8-hour working day, the prohibition of the use of female labour in particularly unhealthy branches of production, 16-week leave for expectant and nursing mothers, and the introduction of the principle of compulsory maternity insurance, etc.[1] Unfortunately this fundamental question that affects directly the interests of every working woman was accorded too little time, and the debates were hurried and abbreviated. Resolutions introducing important addenda to the demands presented by the German delegation were not put forward for debate nor put to the vote, and this despite the fact that the Finnish resolution proposed by Pärssinen, Aalle and Silänpäa and other deputies to the Seim, clearly emphasized a point omitted in the German resolution – the extension of all forms of maternity protection to include both *legitimate* and *illegitimate* mothers, and a review of the laws on infanticide, committed mainly by mothers who have been abandoned to their fate. . . .

It should not be thought that all the measures demanded in the resolution *automatically* covered both legitimate and illegitimate mothers. It is precisely such a fuddled mode of thinking that dominates in the West, sadly even among women socialists, that preference for legalized marital cohabitation, which made it desirable to debate this fundamental point more thoroughly. It was important to emphasize with all the authority of the conference that maternity is to be recognized as a social function independently of the marital and family forms it assumes. . . . The question of principle involved in maternity insurance and protection was, however, submerged in a number of practical details.

Mention must also be made of yet another important omission in the resolution adopted at the conference: it fails to point clearly and precisely to the principle underlying maternal insurance. Is such insurance an independent section of social insurance, or is

[1] A reference to the Fourth Socialist Conference of German Women, which was held in Mannheim on 22-23 September, 1906, and attended by 50 women delegates and 5 women socialists from other countries, including Alexandra Kollontai. The agenda included: the campaign for voting rights for women, propaganda work among rural women, involving domestic servants in the women's movement, etc. On all these issues resolutions were adopted which called for intensification of the struggle for women's rights and satisfaction of their demands.

it merely a subsection of social insurance in case of illness? The formulation of the resolution indicates that those who drew it up viewed maternity insurance as one of the functions to be carried out by hospital bursaries. If this proposition had been more clearly expressed, however, it would undoubtedly have led to an elucidation of certain other propositions, which require closer examination. It would have raised the question of the grounds for extending insurance to cover that large section of the female population not gainfully employed (i.e. the wives of workers) that can still be found in many countries. Is it possible, and is it acceptable to extend insurance to them via their husbands? What is then to be done in the case of 'non-legalized' cohabitation?

A 'simplification' of this complex question in order to avoid debates of principle and heated feelings would scarcely be in the interests of the cause. Despite the adoption of the resolution, the question of maternity insurance cannot be considered as fully dealt with, and Social-Democracy will undoubtedly have to return to it.

More impassioned debate was provoked by the Danish proposal on night work. This resolution, introduced on the initiative of women type-setters, pointed out that legislation prohibiting night work for women but permitting it for men hindered the working woman in her struggle to earn her living. It is only with enormous effort that women succeed in gaining access to better-paid jobs and better working conditions (in printing, for example), and the prohibition on night work for women pushes them back into the ranks of the unskilled workers, exposes them once more to all the temptations of prostitution and the horrors of approaching destitution. Night work must be abolished *simultaneously* for both men and women, as it is equally harmful to both. . . .

The 'over-simplified' way in which the Danish delegates presented the question of night work meant that their resolution was unable to win support. By a majority of 13 votes to 2 (voting was by country) the resolution was rejected. An individual demand meeting the interests of only one specific profession (night work in a skilled profession is found mainly in the printing industry) could not override a demand corresponding to the interests of the class as a whole. However, the conflict this question provoked indicates the need for a serious approach to the question raised by the Danish and Swedish delegations, namely the simultaneous equalizing of the conditions of male and female labour. . . .

The resolution put forward by the chairwoman of the conference, Clara Zetkin, expressing sympathy with Finland, and another resolution put forward by the English, reminding women of their obligation to oppose chauvinism and bring up their children in a spirit of anti-militarism were both adopted without debate and were met with warm applause.[2] The central women's international bureau remained as before in Stuttgart, and *Die Gleichheit* (Equality) was again recognized as the organ of the international socialist movement.

Whatever may have been the superficial failings, of the second international socialist conference, its work will undoubtedly have a major and beneficial influence upon the further success of the workers' movement. There is every reason to hope that the women's socialist movement, which is an integral part of the whole workers' movement, will assume larger and even more impressive dimensions before the next, the third conference. It will also clearly and irrefutably demonstrate that only special propaganda work among the female proletariat, work organized within the party on the basis of technical independence, can supplement the ranks of the organized workers with a 'second army', the army of women workers fighting for the common workers' cause and for the comprehensive emancipation of women.

---

[2] In addition to the resolutions listed above, the international women's conference in Copenhagen also decided to declare 8 March the International Day of Working Women, and to mark it every year as the day of international solidarity among the female proletariat in their struggle for equal economic and political rights. The first International Women's Day was held in 1911 in Germany, Austria, Switzerland and Denmark under the slogan 'Voting rights for women workers so as to unite forces in the struggle for socialism'.

SUMMARY

What is the women's socialist movement, and what are its objectives and aims? What are the forms that it is taking? Is it not simply a branch of bourgeois feminism, its 'left wing'? And if not, how is the existence of separate women's newspapers and magazines, the convocation of meetings, congresses and conferences to be explained? Why is the movement not absorbed into the powerful current of the whole workers' movement?

These questions, which inevitably arise in connection with the women's international socialist conference in Copenhagen in August 1910, frequently cause bewilderment even among socialists, who are, unfortunately, insufficiently familiar with the history of the women's working-class movement in the West.

The history of this movement, however, is instructive and to a certain extent provides the answer to such questions.

Today there is hardly a socialist who would openly dispute the importance of the organization of women workers and the desirability of creating a broad women's socialist movement. Socialists now take pride in the size of the 'women's army' and, when estimating the chances of success in the process of class struggle, take into account this new and rapidly increasing active force. However, there was a time, and not all that long ago – about 25 years – when such a thing as a *women's socialist movement* had never been heard of in any country, even if it had hundreds of thousands, millions, of women workers.

When, 14 years ago, during the international congress held in London in 1896, 30 women delegates (from England, Germany, America, Holland, Belgium and Poland) arranged for their own separate women's conference, only a couple of countries (Germany, England) were making their first attempts to set up a women's socialist movement. The workers' organizations in every country did, it is true, include individual women in their ranks, but, on entering the ranks of the party and taking part in the trade union struggle, the majority of these women as it was renounced in advance their work on behalf of the most deprived and legally unprotected section of the working class – women workers. Virtually nothing was being done by the party to raise the class consciousness of working women, for the emancipation of women as housewives and mothers.

This was the situation in Germany until the beginning of the 1890s, in England and other countries until the beginning of the 20th century, and in Russia up to the revolutionary upheavals of 1905. In those countries where organizations of working women assumed primarily a professional form (for example, England and America), work was conducted in the main together with the bourgeois feminists and under their direct leadership; there was no question of a class struggle.

The first unofficial conference of women socialist delegates held in London in 1896 concerned itself mainly with an examination of the relationship between bourgeois feminism and the women's proletarian movement. It was recognized as desirable to distinguish between the women's bourgeois movement and the women's socialist movement, and emphasis was placed upon the urgent need to intensify socialist propaganda work among working women in order to involve them in the class struggle.

Eleven years have passed since then. Capitalism has continued its successful progress, developing itself to the full and subordinating to itself not only new branches of production, but also new countries. Female labour has become a major social force within the national economy. However it was precisely women workers, outside any organization, not linked to their class comrades by any obligations, dispersed and isolated from one another, who were in effect dangerous and damaging rivals of the male section of the working class, often undermining the successes the latter had achieved by active demonstrations.

The question of organizing women workers and of the ways and means of involving them in the general movement became an urgent and immediate issue. Feeling their way, adapting to the conditions in their country, the worker organizations in different countries attempted, each using its own methods, to solve this problem. The result was a variegated and motley scene. The forms taken by the women's proletarian movement varied according to local conditions. However, the most important thing was that the movement of the women of the working class had been called into being – it existed.

By 1907 the movement had assumed such a scale that it was possible to convene the first international women's conference in Stuttgart. When the representatives from the various countries revealed what they had achieved in their own countries, the results, if not impressive of themselves, held promise in terms of the possibilities opened up for the future. There now emerged the question of the formation of an international women's bureau to coordinate the women's socialist organizations in different countries. The bureau was set up in Stuttgart, and the magazine *Die Gleichheit* (Equality) was recognized as the central organ of the international movement.

The conference held in Stuttgart was of decisive importance for the socialist movement. It secured for the movement that independence which it needed for the future success of its work. It became clear that the women's proletarian movement was an integral part of the whole movement of the working class. Nonetheless, the specific social and political position of women in contemporary society requires that a particular approach be adopted towards women, and puts before the party a number of special objectives. These objectives, while they form *part* of the whole working-class movement, while they form part of the common aim, nonetheless affect specifically female interests more closely and are therefore more properly pursued by the *women representatives of the working class themselves*. This point of view has now prevailed, but its elaboration nonetheless required great effort on the part of the women, and provoked a sharp conflict of opinions. . . .

The German party was the first to conduct independent propaganda work among the female proletariat; other countries gradually followed its example. The seeds sown by the first supporters of the women's socialist movement led by Clara Zetkin are already taking root. . . .

Over recent years efforts have been made everywhere to arouse the awareness of working-class women by drawing them into the party. Everywhere the movement is carrying out painstaking work to involve working women in the broad current of the whole movement. . . . The reports made by different countries at the women's conference in Copenhagen is proof of this tireless activity.

How this meeting of almost 100 representatives of the working class of 17 countries differed from the usual bourgeois congresses of suffragettes! . . .

After two days of animated and enthusiastic work, the delegates to the second socialist women's conference left the hall of the hospitable People's House imbued with the firm belief that by the third international conference of socialist women, the 'second army' of the working class in every country will be able to swell its ranks with a fresh inflow of new and active forces from among the women of the working class.

[*A Third International Women's Conference had been planned for Vienna in 1914, but it was prevented by the outbreak of the Great War.*]

## 'WOMEN'S DAY'
*PRAVDA*
23 February (8 March) 1913

What is 'Women's Day'? Is it really necessary? Is it not a concession to the women of the bourgeois class, to the feminists and suffragettes? Is it not harmful to the unity of the workers' movement?

Such questions can still be heard in Russia, though they are no longer heard abroad. Life itself has already supplied a clear and eloquent answer.

'Women's Day' is a link in the long, solid chain of the women's proletarian movement. The organized army of working women grows with every year. Twenty years ago the trade unions contained only small groups of working women scattered here and there among the ranks of the workers' party.... Now English trade unions have over 292,000 women members; in Germany around 200,000 are in the trade union movement and 150,000 in the workers' party, and in Austria there are 47,000 in the trade unions and almost 20,000 in the party. Everywhere – in Italy, Hungary, Denmark, Sweden, Norway and Switzerland – the women of the working class are organizing themselves. The women's socialist army has almost a million members. A powerful force! A force that the powers of this world must reckon with when it is a question of the cost of living, maternity insurance, child labour and legislation to protect female labour.

There was a time when working men thought that they alone must bear on their shoulders the brunt of the struggle against capital, that they alone must deal with the 'old world' without the help of their womenfolk. However, as working-class women entered the ranks of those who sell their labour, forced onto the labour market by need, by the fact that husband or father is unemployed, working men became aware that to leave women behind in the ranks of the 'non-class-conscious' was to damage their cause and hold it back. The greater the number of conscious fighters, the greater the chances of success. What level of consciousness is possessed by a woman who sits by the stove, who has no rights in society, the state or the family? She has no 'ideas' of her own! Everything is done as ordered by the father or husband. . . .

The backwardness and lack of rights suffered by women, their subjection and indifference, are of no benefit to the working class, and indeed are directly harmful to it. But how is the woman worker to be drawn into the movement, how is she to be awoken?

Social-Democracy abroad did not find the correct solution immediately. Workers' organizations were open to women workers, but only a few entered. Why? Because the working class at first did not realize that the woman worker is the most legally and socially deprived member of that class, that she has been browbeaten, intimidated, persecuted down the centuries, and that in order to stimulate her mind and heart, a special approach is needed, words understandable to her as a woman. The workers did not immediately appreciate that in this world of lack of rights and exploitation, the woman is oppressed not only as a seller of her labour, but also as a mother, as a woman. . . . However, when the workers' socialist party understood this, it boldly took up the defence of women on both counts as a hired worker and as a woman, a mother.

Socialists in every country began to demand special protection for female labour, insurance for mother and child, political rights for women and the defence of women's interests.

The more clearly the workers' party perceived this second objective vis-à-vis women workers, the more willingly women joined the party, the more they appreciated that the party is their true champion, that the working class is struggling also for their urgent and exclusively female needs. Working women themselves, organized and conscious, have done a great deal to elucidate this objective. Now the main burden of the work to attract more working women into the socialist movement lies with the women. The parties in every country have their own special women's committees, secretariats and bureaus. These women's committees conduct work among the still largely non-politically conscious female population, arouse the consciousness of working women and organize them. They also examine those questions and demands that affect women most closely: protection and provision for expectant and nursing mothers, the legislative regulation of female labour, the campaign against prostitution and infant mortality, the demand for political rights for women, the improvement of housing, the campaign against the rising cost of living, etc.

Thus, as members of the party, women workers are fighting for the common class cause, while at the same time outlining and putting forward those needs and demands that most nearly affect themselves as women, housewives and mothers. The party supports these demands and fights for them. . . . The requirements of working women are part and parcel of the common workers' cause!

On 'Women's Day' the organized demonstrate against their lack of rights.

But, some will say, why this *singling out* of women workers? Why special 'Women's Days', special leaflets for working women, meetings and conferences of working-class women? Is this not, in the final analysis, a concession to the feminists and bourgeois suffragettes?

Only those who do not understand the radical difference between the movement of socialist women and bourgeois suffragettes can think this way.

What is the aim of the feminists? Their aim is to achieve the same advantages, the same power, the same rights within capitalist society as those possessed now by their husbands, fathers and brothers. What is the aim of the women workers? Their aim is to abolish all privileges deriving from birth or wealth. For the woman worker it is a matter of indifference who is the 'master' a man or a woman. Together with the whole of her class, she can ease her position as a worker.

Feminists demand equal rights always and everywhere. Women workers reply: we demand rights for every citizen, man and woman, but we are not prepared to forget that we are not only workers and citizens, but also mothers! And as mothers, as women who give birth to the future, we demand special concern for ourselves and our children, special protection from the state and society.

The feminists are striving to acquire political rights. However, here too our paths separate.

For bourgeois women, political rights are simply a means allowing them to make their way more conveniently and more securely in a world founded on the exploitation of the working people. For women workers, political rights are a step along the rocky and difficult path that leads to the desired kingdom of labour.

The paths pursued by women workers and bourgeois suffragettes have long since separated. There is too great a difference between the objectives that life has put before them. There is too great a contradiction between the interests of the woman worker and the lady proprietress, between the servant and her mistress. . . . There are not and cannot be any points of contact, conciliation or convergence between them. Therefore working men should not fear separate Women's Days, nor special conferences of women workers, nor their special press.

Every special, distinct form of work among the women of the working class is simply a means of arousing the consciousness of the woman worker and drawing her into the ranks of those fighting for a better future. . . . Women's Days and the slow, meticulous work undertaken to arouse the self-consciousness of the woman worker are serving the cause not of the division but of the unification of the working class.

Let a joyous sense of serving the common class cause and of fighting simultaneously for their own female emancipation inspire women workers to join in the celebration of Women's Day.

# PART 2

# THE RUSSIAN REVOLUTION

## 'OUR TASKS'

*RABOTNITSA*

1917


A serious task of great responsibility now faces the working men and women of our country. We must build the new Russia, a Russia in which the working people, office workers, servants, day workers, needlewomen and those who are simply the wives of working men, will have a better and brighter life than they had during the accursed reign of bloody Nicholas.

However, the task of winning and consolidating state power for the proletariat and the small peasant, of introducing and implementing such legislation as will limit the appetites of capitalist exploiters and defend the interests of workers, is not the only task now facing the working men and women of Russia. The proletariat of Russia now occupies a special position *vis-à-vis* the working men and women of other countries.

The great Russian revolution has placed us, Russian working men and women, in the front ranks of those fighting for the worldwide workers' cause, for the interests of all workers.

We are able to speak, write and act more freely than the working women and men of other countries.

How, then, can we not use this freedom, won for us by the blood of our comrades, to concentrate our forces, the forces of the women of the working class, without delay in order to conduct a tireless, insistent mass struggle to achieve the quickest possible end to world war?

Our women comrades, the working women of other countries, are waiting for us to take this step.

War is now the most dreadful evil hanging over us. While the war continues we cannot build the new Russia, cannot resolve the problem of bread, of food, cannot halt the rising cost of living.

While, with every hour that passes, the war continues to kill and cripple our children and husbands, we, the women of the working class, cannot know peace! . . .

If our first task is to help our comrades build the new, democratic Russia, our second task, no less urgent, and closer to our hearts, is to rouse working women to declare war on war.

And this means: firstly, not only to ourselves understand that this is not our war, that it is being waged in the name of the pecuniary interests of the wealthy bosses, bankers and manufacturers, but also to constantly explain this to our working comrades both women and men.

Secondly, it means uniting the forces of working women and men around that party which not only defends the interests of the Russian proletariat, but is also fighting to ensure that proletarian blood is not shed for the glory of capitalists.

Comrade women workers! We can no longer resign ourselves to war and rising prices! We must fight. Join our ranks, the ranks of the Social-Democratic Labour Party! However, it is not enough to join the party. If we really want to hasten peace, then working men and women must fight to ensure that state power is transferred from the hands of big capitalists – the ones really responsible for all our woes, all the blood being shed on battlefields – to the hands of our representatives, the Soviet of Workers' and Soldiers' Deputies.

In the struggle against war and rising prices, in the struggle to secure power in Russia for the dispossessed, for the working people, in the struggle for a new order and new laws, much depends on us, the women workers. The days are passed when the success of the workers' cause depended only on the organization of the men. Now, as a result of this war, there has been a sharp change in the position of working-class women. Female labour can now be found everywhere. War has forced women to take jobs that before they would never have thought of. Whereas in 1912 there were only 45 women for every 100 men working in factories, now it is not uncommon to find 100 women for every 75 men.

The success of the workers' cause, the success of the workers' struggle for a better life – for a shorter working day, for higher pay, for health insurance, unemployment pay, old-age pensions, etc. – the success of their struggle to defend the work of our children, to obtain better schools, now depends not only on the consciousness and organization of the men, but also on the number of women workers entering the ranks of the organized working class. The more of us enter the ranks of the organized fighters for our common workers' cause and needs, the sooner we will win concessions from the capitalist extortionists.

All our strength, all our hope, lies in organization!

Now our slogan must be: comrade women workers! Do not stand in isolation. Isolated, we are but straws that any boss can bend to his will, but organized we are a mighty force that no one can break.

We, the women workers, were the first to raise the Red Banner in the days of the Russian revolution, the first to go out onto the streets on Women's Day. Let us now hasten to join the leading ranks of the fighters for the workers' cause, let us join trade unions, the Social-Democratic Party, the Soviet of Workers' and Soldiers' Deputies!

Our ranks united, we will aim at rapidly putting an end to bloody war among the nations; we will oppose all who have forgotten the great working-class precept of unity, of solidarity among the workers of every country.

It is only in revolutionary struggle against the capitalists of every country, and only in union with the working women and men of the whole world, that we will achieve a new and brighter future – the socialist brotherhood of the workers.

A great and long-awaited event which we Marxists always believed to be inevitable, but which we nonetheless viewed rather as a dream or an ideal of the future rather than as an imminent reality, has at last occurred. [October Revolution.]

The Russian proletariat, supported by armed soldiers - and they too are the sons of proletarians or peasants – have seized state power. For the first time in the history of man a state is headed not by the representatives of capital, of the bourgeoisie, but by the vanguard of the fighting proletariat – the left wing of Russian Social-Democracy, the Bolsheviks.

As far back as the February revolution, in Russia, the Bolsheviks realized the inevitability of a clash between the working class, supported by an exhausted peasantry and soldiers wearied to death of war, and the Russian bourgeoisie.

All that the February revolution of 1917 achieved was the overthrow of tsarism and the introduction of those commonly accepted political rights and freedoms recognized by any liberal-bourgeois government (freedom of association and the press, the right to coalition and alliance). The old, bureaucratic, bourgeois spirit that reigned over life in Russia remained unchanged. The former officials remained in all the ministries, the former laws and regulations continued to operate throughout the land, and the only difference was that the former monarchists became the faithful servants first of Milyukov and Guchkov, and then of Kerensky and Tereshchenko.

The major capitalists and industrialists in Russia thought that after the February revolution the danger was past, and that after the overthrow of the tsarist regime, capitalists in Russia would have full freedom of action in order to create in Russia a purely capitalist republic similar to the one in Northern America, where all state power is firmly in the hands of capitalist magnates. Only this summer the Russian bourgeoisie celebrated its victory, and sought by every kind of political intrigue and deceit (and in particular by the formation of a coalition government) to strengthen its position and weaken that of the socialists. It sought to buy over wavering social-patriots such as Tsereteli, Chernov and Avksentyev by promising them a share in government.

At that time there existed in Russia only one party which, from the very beginning of the February revolution, adopted a negative attitude towards the bourgeois-imperialist policies of the Cadets and social-patriots – *and that was the Bolshevik Party*. As far back as April the Bolsheviks put forward the slogan: 'All power to the Soviets!' and repeatedly emphasized that it was essential to end the war. However, the war could only be ended by revolution and the overthrow of the bourgeois-capitalist government. Therefore, anyone who wanted to fight for peace had, at the same time, to fight to seize power. The more resolutely the Bolsheviks supported these slogans, the more savagely they were attacked by their political opponents, by the Cadets and their lackeys from the socialist party – the social-patriots. But the Bolsheviks calmly continued their work, fulfilling their great historical mission.

The Bolsheviks not only found themselves in opposition, flaying the social-patriots and ceaselessly criticizing and exposing the harmful essence of imperialism both within and without Russia, but they also sought energetically and persistently to create a basis for the development of a revolutionary workers' movement that would be supported by the popular masses and would not hesitate before open and armed insurrection.

In Petrograd, Moscow and throughout Russia large trade unions were formed with 100 to 200,000 members (metal workers, textile workers, wood workers, etc.). Then under the leadership of the

Bolsheviks, workers' and soldiers' clubs were set up with their own libraries, study courses, cheap canteens, etc. At the same time, the first steps were taken to organize a union of socialist youth, whose membership reached 50,000. The Bolsheviks also did a great deal of work among the soldiers at the front in order to strengthen the spirit of internationalism there also. Millions of copies of pamphlets and brochures were distributed which openly set out the problem of war as understood by socialist-internationalists. Bolshevik-led meetings, congresses and conferences were also called for the same purpose.

However, if the Bolsheviks prepared the way for the October Revolution by means of active propaganda and organizational work, it must not be forgotten that it was the *objective conditions themselves which created the ground for this second revolution.*

The February revolution could remove none of the factors which caused it, namely war, rising prices, famine and privation. At the same time, the Russian bourgeoisie calmly continued their rule.

In July the reactionary trend in the policy of the bourgeoisie (the Cadets) was becoming increasingly obvious. The workers' press was banned, Bolsheviks were arrested, and the death penalty was reintroduced for soldiers.

Then came the notorious plot between General Kornilov and the Cadet leaders. From September onwards there were signs of an approaching and increasingly bitter struggle between revolutionary democracy and the liberal bourgeoisie. Now the question was: to whom should republican Russia belong – to the capitalists, or to the workers and poor peasants? The soldiers, weary to death of war, were inclining more and more towards the Bolsheviks, while the Kerensky government was increasingly aggressive. . . .

The dictatorship of the bourgeois parties, or the struggle for the dictatorship of the proletariat – that was the question facing the Second Congress of Soviets of Workers' and Soldiers' Deputies which met in Petrograd on 25 October (old style).

The people came out victorious without either a hard struggle or much bloodshed. The Soviets of Workers took power into their hands. Not one soldier, not one sailor, not one worker supported the government of Kerensky. Only individual groups from the bourgeois camp supported the government. The Congress of Soviets declared: that which we have waited for so long has happened - state power is in the hands of revolutionary democracy, i.e. in the hands of the workers, the poor peasants, the soldiers and sailors! As was to be expected, the first step taken by a truly socialist government was the proclamation of the Decree on Peace.

The People's Commissars immediately set about implementing the programme of the working class. A new spirit emerged. All the old bureaucratic methods and customs were swept away. Self-administration and the principle of election came into operation throughout the country for all posts, including those in the armed forces (even commanders are elected and appointed by the soldiers). All of this is now characteristic of life in Russia.

The new socialist government, the government of workers and peasants, is now taking energetic measures to restore the national economy, finances and industry, which have been totally destroyed. However, even more could have been achieved if it had not been for the bourgeoisie, which looked with hatred and anger at the rule of the 'mob' and did all it could to impede the new work of creation. One example of this is the notorious 'sabotage' by state employees in all the ministries, in state institutions, and even in schools and hospitals. Teachers, doctors, journalists, the whole of the intelligentsia, opposed the workers, the socialist state. As soon as a People's Commissar took office, all state employees immediately, like experienced strikers, stopped work, leaving ministries and other institutions empty. Many schools and hospitals had to be closed as a result of strikes among the teaching and medical staff.

The elderly and orphans were thrown out of the refuges where they had found shelter because the staff refused to accept money to support these institutions from a 'socialist Bolshevik government'! . . .

Often, when the staff left the ministries, they took with them not only all the documents, but also the keys of the safes and all the money.

Is it therefore surprising that the socialist government, faced with such an unprecedented boycott and sabotage, affecting so adversely innocent members of society, adopted rigorous measures against Cadets and liberals?

However, despite all these difficulties, the Bolshevik government continued its constructive work. Radical social reforms were implemented. Concern was shown for the poorest and most deprived members of the population. Particular care was shown towards those injured during the war. A campaign was mounted against unemployment. Reforms were also carried through in the administration of justice. Severe measures were taken against speculation. Particular attention was paid to school education, and efforts were made to deal with the housing crisis.

It is not at all surprising, therefore, if such policies defending the interests of the masses provoke different reactions to the socialist government among different sections of society. On the one hand, the socialist government faces the hatred, slander and anger of the whole bourgeois class, while, on the other hand, it arouses admiration, genuine devotion and resolute support amongst the workers, soldiers and peasants.

Revolutionary democracy clearly understands and feels that the Bolshevik government is the only correct organ of power for new, democratic Russia. Either Russia will become a bourgeois-capitalist republic (should the Cadets come to power), or under the leadership of the proletariat, it will develop as a purely democratic republic and will gradually create new forms for the national economy and social relations.

Following the October Revolution in Russia, the slogan 'the dictatorship of the proletariat' is no longer a utopia but a reality which all the bourgeois classes in other countries must reckon with. The Russian revolution marked only the beginning of the great struggle to liberate the proletariat from the yoke of capitalism. It is of vital importance for the proletariat of every country that the Bolsheviks should emerge from this struggle victorious. This victory will also deal a lethal blow to world imperialism.

## 'DECREE ON CHILD WELFARE'
## 1918

Two million young lives were yearly dwindling in Russia because of the darkness of the oppressed people, because of apathy of the class state. Two million suffering mothers were saturating yearly the Russian earth with tears and were covering with their blistered hands the early graves of the innocent victims of the hideous social order. The human thought, which had for centuries sought a path, has at last reached the bright epoch of workers' reforms, which will safeguard the mother for the child and the child for the mother. What is capitalist morality: homes for orphans filled above capacity, having a colossal mortality rate and a hideous form of nursing the infants, which form was an insult to the sacred feelings of a helpless labouring mother and which made the mother-citizen a dull nursing animal. All these horrors of a nightmare have fortunately, sunk in the dark mist of the past since the victory of the workers and the peasants. A morning, bright and pure for the children themselves has come.

You, working women, labouring mother-citizens, with your responsive hearts, – you brave builders of the new social life, – you ideal pedagogues, children's physicians and nurses, – all of you are called by the new Soviet Russia to contribute your minds and feelings to the building of the great structure of social welfare of the future generations. All the small and large institutions of the Commissariat of Social Welfare which serve the children, – all of them from the day of publication of this decree, mould into one state organization and are transformed to the supervision of the Department for safeguarded mothers and children, so as to create an inseparable chain together with the Institutions for the care of pregnant women, for the purpose of bringing up mentally and physically strong citizens. The Petrograd Home with all the auxiliary branches, becomes part of the 'Palace for Safeguarding Motherhood and Infancy', as one of its departments and is named 'The Palace of Infancy'. The Moscow Home becomes part of the Moscow Institute of Motherhood and is named 'The Moscow Institute of Infancy'.

For the purpose of precipitating the realization of the necessary reforms for the safeguarding of childhood in Russia, at the Department for Safeguarding Motherhood and Infancy a Committee is being organized. It is to be composed of representatives of the Soviet of Workers', Soldiers' and Peasants' Deputies, of Workers' organizations and of specialists, interested in the question of social welfare of the infants. The following principles are to be the Committee's guiding principles:

1. Safeguarding the mother for the child: the best drop of milk for the child – is the milk from its mother's breast.

2. Bring up the child in an atmosphere of a widely developed Socialist family.

3. To create for the child conditions, which would lay a foundation for the development of its physical and mental strength and for bright understanding of life.

People's Commissar: A. Kollontai.
Member of the Collegium, supervising the Department for Safeguarding Motherhood and Infancy: N. Korcleff.
Sect'y: Zvetkoff.
January 31, 1918.

## 'WHAT ARE WE FIGHTING FOR?'
1919

This is a question that disturbs many, the question that faces the Red Army and the workers, and troubles the peasants. Did not the Communist-Bolsheviks, two years ago, summon us in the name of peace? Why does war continue? Why are we being mobilized yet again and sent to the front?

In order to answer this question one must understand what is happening all around us, the events that are taking place. As soon as the workers and peasants took power into their hands in October, 1917, they honestly and openly offered peace to all the peoples. However, the workers in the other countries were still too weak, and the predatory capitalists were still strong enough to continue the war. In March, 1918, the Soviet government, desirous of peace, signed the disadvantageous and onerous Brest Peace Treaty with Germany in order to return the ploughman to the field, the worker to his lathe, in order to save the lives of its free citizens.

However, the imperialist predators are not afraid of blood, and place no value on human life. They needed war, and therefore the bourgeoisie of every country mounted repeated attacks upon Soviet Russia and the Soviet Ukraine from outside, while inside the country they encouraged kulak action against the workers and peasants. A new battle front took shape – not Russians against Germans or Ukrainians against the allies, but 'Reds' against 'Whites', i.e. the working people against the bourgeoisie.

What else could the people do? Should they say: We are against war, we are for peace, and therefore, if the Kolchaks, Denikins and Krasnovs attack us, we will not take up arms?! Let American, or German or Russian capital rule over us once more and introduce amongst us the system that suits it best – it's all the same to us?!

Of course, not one rationally-minded Red Army soldier, worker or peasant would say anything of the kind.

The peasant soon realizes: if Skoropadsky returns, together with the priests and the landowners, it will be farewell to land and freedom! Once more it will be doff your cap before the village policeman and starve to death while the landowners' barns burst with golden grain!

The worker would understand that the return to power of the bourgeoisie would mean a return to lack of rights, to the exploitation of labour, the abolition of the 8-hour working day and unemployment benefit, that it would lead to the expulsion of the working people from their light and healthy flats to be chased back into damp cellars. It would mean a return to the slavery of hired labour.

The Red Army soldier would remember the prison-like regime of the tsarist barracks, blows by officers, insult and abuse from commanders of the old order, rotten meat for dinner, theft by military superintendents, and his hands would seek instinctively for his protecting rifle.

All the working people taken as a whole cannot fail to understand that now the question is whether the peasants and workers are to be the masters of Russia and the Ukraine, or whether the priests, landowners and capitalists are to return and hang once more like a millstone around the neck of the people.

This is not war, but the working people rising up in defence of their rights, freedom and very life!

We are fighting not in order to annex new lands or enslave or plunder another people, but in order to safeguard ourselves from the capitalist predators. We are fighting in order to secure for the peasant and his children the possibility of peacefully farming the land, in order to give the worker the possibility not only of working at a factory or plant, but of himself participating in the organization of production, himself distributing the national wealth in such a way that each gets his just due, rather than one man getting it all simply because he is a capitalist and takes for himself the lion's share of the national wealth.

We are fighting in order to defend the right of the workers and peasants to run their own homeland. We are fighting in order to protect the people against the possible return of famine and rising prices. We are fighting in order to create one, united, international fraternal republic of workers and peasants, destroy private-property owners and the predatory rich, and thus put an end to war once and for all.

Our war – the war of the Reds against the Whites – is the revolt of the oppressed against those who are responsible for bloodshed. Our cry is and will remain 'War on war! Long live peaceful productive labour on behalf of all working people!'

Bulletin of the Kharkov Soviet
and the Provincial Executive Committee
of the Soviets of Workers',
Peasants' and Red Army Deputies,
7 May 1919

## 'ON THE HISTORY OF THE MOVEMENT
## OF WOMEN WORKERS IN RUSSIA'
1920

What year could be said to mark the beginning of the working women's movement in Russia? In its essential nature, the movement of women workers is inseparably linked with the entire proletarian movement as one indivisible whole. The woman worker, as a member of the proletarian class, as someone selling her labour, also rose in revolt with the workers every time they opposed the violation of their human rights, participated together and on an equal footing with the workers in all worker uprisings, in all the factory revolts so hated by tsarism.

For this reason, the beginning of the movement of women workers in Russia coincides with the first signs of the awakening of class self-consciousness among the Russian proletariat, and with its first attempts, by means of combined pressure, strikes and walk-outs, to achieve more tolerable, less humiliating and miserly conditions of existence.

Women workers took active part in the worker revolts at the Krenholm factory in 1872 and at the Lazeryev textile factory in Moscow in 1874. They were involved in the strike in 1878 at the New Cotton-Spinning Plant in Petrograd and led the weavers' strike in the famous workers' demonstration in Orekhovo-Zuyevo, during which factory buildings were wrecked. As a result, the tsarist government was compelled to hurry through its legislation prohibiting night work for women and children, which came into force on 3 June, 1885.

It is indicative that the spontaneous wave of strikes that shook proletarian Russia in the 1870s and the early 1880s affected mainly the textile industry, in which the majority of the work force is made up of cheap female labour. The disturbances of the 1870s and early 1880s occurred for purely economic reasons, provoked by unemployment and the continuing crisis in the cotton industry. However, is it not remarkable that this downtrodden 'factory girl', without rights, oppressed by labour beyond her strength and politically ignorant, despised even by the female half of the urban petty bourgeoisie and held at arm's length by peasant women who clung tenaciously to old traditions, should be in the front ranks of those fighting for the rights of the working class, for the emancipation of women? The harsh conditions of life itself compelled the factory girl to oppose openly the power of the bosses and the enslavement of capital. However, in fighting for the rights and interests of her class, the woman worker was unwittingly also preparing the way for the emancipation of women from those chains that still weighed upon them in particular and created inequality of status and conditions among men and women workers, even within the framework of one single working class.

During the new and intensified wave of worker disturbances in the mid- and the late 1890s, working women were once again invariably active participants in worker revolts. The April revolt at the Yaroslavl factory in 1895 received vigorous support from the women weavers. Nor were women workers less active than their male comrades during the economic strikes of 1894-1895 in St. Petersburg. When, in the summer of 1896, St. Petersburg became the scene of the historic strike by textile workers, the women weavers courageously and unanimously walked out of the workshops together with the men weavers. What difference does it make that at home hungry children are waiting for their working mother? What difference does it make that this strike brings with it the threat of dismissal, of exile or prison? The common class cause is more important, more sacred than maternal feelings, concern for the family, for personal and family well-being!

At a time of disturbances and strikes the woman worker, oppressed, timid, without rights, straightens up to her full height and becomes equal as a fighter and comrade. This transformation takes place unconsciously, spontaneously, but it is important and significant. It is the path along which the workers' movement is leading the woman worker to liberation, not only as one who sells her labour, but also as a woman, a wife, a mother and a housewife.

At the end of the 1890s and the beginning of the 20th century there were a number of disturbances and strikes at factories employing mainly women: at tobacco-processing factories (Shanshai), at spinning and weaving mills (Maxwell) in Petrograd, etc. The working-class movement in Russia is gaining strength, organizing itself, taking shape. So also is class resistance among the female proletariat.

Nonetheless, until the momentous year of the first Russian revolution the movement was basically economic in nature. Political slogans had to be concealed or advanced in disguised form. A healthy class instinct prompts the woman worker to support strikes, and not infrequently the women themselves organize and carry through 'factory revolts'. However, no sooner had the wave of bitter strike struggle passed, no sooner had the workers returned to work, victorious or defeated, than the women were once again isolated from one another, still unconscious of the need for organization, for constant comradely contact. In those years it was still exceptional to find a woman worker in the illegal party organizations. The broad objectives of the socialist workers' party had still not seized hold of the working woman, and she remained unresponsive to universal political slogans. The life led by six million proletarian women in Russia at the beginning of the 20th century was still too dark, too unenlightened, and their existence too much in the grip of hunger, deprivation and humiliation. A 12-hour, or at best an 11-hour working day, a starvation wage of 12-15 roubles a month, accommodation in overcrowded barracks, the absence of any form of assistance from the state or society in case of illness, pregnancy or unemployment, the impossibility of organizing self-help as the tsarist government savagely persecuted any attempts at organization by the workers – these were the conditions surrounding the woman worker. Her back was bent by the intolerable burden of oppression, and her soul, terrified by the spectre of poverty and starvation, refused to believe in a brighter future and the possibility of fighting to cast off the yoke of tsarism and capital.

At the beginning of the 20th century, women workers avoided politics and revolutionary struggle. The socialist movement in Russia can, it is true, take pride in an abundance of charming and heroic women who, by their energetic work and selflessness, helped to consolidate the underground movement and prepared the way for the revolutionary explosion that occurred in the years that followed. However none of these women, from the first women socialists such as Sofia Bardina or the Leshern sisters, full of charm and inner beauty, to the iron-willed Sofia Perovskaya, were representatives of the female proletariat. In the majority of cases these were the young girls to which Turgenev dedicated his prose poem 'The Threshold', girls from a wealthy, aristocratic background who left their parental homes, broke with their prosperous past and 'went to the people' to spread revolutionary propaganda and fight against social injustice, striving to redeem the 'sins of their fathers'. Even much later, in the 1890s and the beginning of the 20th century, when Marxism had already put down deep roots in the Russian workers' movement, the number of women workers involved in the movement was very small. The active women members of the underground organizations in those years were not women workers but women from the intelligentsia – students, teachers, medical assistants and writers. It was rare to find a 'factory girl' at an illegal meeting. Nor did the women workers attend the Sunday evening classes held just outside the city limits of Petrograd, which were then the only legal method of spreading, under the innocent guise of geography or arithmetic, the ideas of Marxism and scientific socialism among the broad working masses. Working women still fought shy of life, avoided combat . . . still believed that their lot was the oven, the wash-tub and the cradle.

THE FIRST REVOLUTION OF 1905

The picture changes radically from the moment when the red spectre of revolution first overshadowed Russia with its fiery wings. The revolutionary year of 1905 sent deep shock waves through the working masses. The Russian worker sensed his strength for the first time, for the first time realized that he was bearing on his shoulders the whole national wealth. The Russian proletarian woman worker, the unfailing collaborator in all the political demonstrations of the proletariat in the revolutionary years of 1905-1906, was also awoken from her slumbers. She was to be found everywhere. If we wanted to relate the facts of the mass participation of women in the movement of the time, enumerate all the active manifestations of protest and struggle by women workers, recall all the selfless actions undertaken by proletarian women, their loyalty to the ideals of socialism, then we would have to reconstruct scene by scene the entire history of the Russian revolution of 1905.

Many still remember those years full of romanticism. The image of the woman worker, still 'incomplete', but already stirring into life, with her searching, hope-filled eyes turned on the speaker at crowded meetings charged with infectious enthusiasm, lives once again in the memory. The faces of women, filled with concentrated energy and unshakable resolution, can be seen among the serried ranks of the workers' procession on the memorial on the memorable 9 January, bloody Sunday. A sun, unusually bright for St. Petersburg, illuminates this purposeful, solemn and silent procession, highlighting the women's faces, so numerous among the crowd. The penalty for naive illusions and childish trustfulness strikes the women; the woman worker, young girl, working wife, is a common figure among the mass victims of that January day. The slogan 'General Strike' that flies from workshop to workshop is picked up by these women, yesterday still lacking class consciousness, and compels some of them to be the first to walk out.

The women workers in the provinces did not lag behind their comrades in the capital. In the October days, exhausted by work and their harsh existence on the edge of starvation, women leave the factories and, in the name of the common cause, courageously deprive their children of their last piece of bread. . . . With simple, moving words the woman worker appeals to her male comrades, suggesting that they too leave their work; she keeps up the spirits of those on strike, breathing energy into those who waver. . . . The woman worker struggled tirelessly, protested courageously, sacrificed herself heroically for the common cause, and the more active she became, the more rapidly was the process of her mental awakening achieved. The woman worker began to take note of the world around her, of the injustices stemming from the capitalist system. She became more painfully and acutely aware of the bitterness of all her sufferings and sorrows. Alongside common proletarian demands one can hear ever more distinctly the voices of the women of the working class recalling the needs and requirements of women workers. At the time of the elections to the Shidlovsky commission in March, 1905, the refusal to admit women as worker delegates provoked murmurs of discontent among women: the sufferings and sacrifices that they had only recently passed through had brought the men and women of the working class closer together, put them on an equal footing. It appeared particularly unjust at that moment to turn to the woman fighter and citizen and underline her age-old lack of rights. When the Shidlovsky commission refused to recognize the woman chosen as one of the seven delegates from the Sampsoniyevsky textile works, the indignant women workers representing several textile works decided to present to the commission the following protest declaration: 'Women deputies representing women workers are not allowed onto the commission under your chairmanship. We believe such a decision to be unjust. Women workers predominate in the factories and mills of St. Petersburg. The number of women employed in spinning and weaving mills is increasing every year because the men are moving to factories that offer better pay. We, the women workers, bear a heavier burden of work. Because of our helplessness and lack of rights, we are kept down more by our comrades, and paid less. When this commission was announced, our hearts filled with hope; at last the time is coming – we thought – when the woman worker in St Petersburg will be able to speak out to the whole of Russia in the name of all her sister workers about the oppression, wrongs and humiliations of which the male worker can know nothing. And then, when we had already chosen our deputies, we were informed that only men can be deputies. However, we hope that this is not your final decision. . . .'

The refusal to allow women workers the right of representation and their expulsion from political life constituted a blatant injustice for all that section of the female population that had carried on its shoulders the burden of the liberation struggle. Women workers repeatedly attended pre-election meetings during the election campaigns for the First and Second Dumas, and noisily protested against a law that deprived them of any voice in a matter so important as the election of a representative to the Russian parliament. There were instances, for example in Moscow, when women workers came to meetings of electors, broke up the meeting and protested against the way the elections were being conducted.

That women workers were no longer indifferent to their lack of rights is also shown by the fact that, of the 40,000 signatures on petitions addressed to the First and Second State Dumas demanding that electoral rights be extended to women also, a large majority were those of women workers. The collection of signatures was organized by the Alliance for Female Equality and other bourgeois women's organizations, and was conducted at plants and factories. The fact that women workers willingly signed petitions drawn up by bourgeois women also reveals that the political consciousness of women workers was only just awakening, that they were taking their first, hesitant steps, still stopping half-way. The women workers were becoming aware of their deprivation and lack of political rights, but were still unable to link this fact with the common struggle of their own class, were unable to find the correct path that would lead proletarian women to their full and comprehensive emancipation. The woman worker still naively accepted the hand held out to her by bourgeois feminists. The suffragettes turned to the working women, hoping to draw them onto their side, get their support and organize them into purely feminine, supposedly non-class, but essentially bourgeois alliances. However, a healthy class instinct and a deep mistrust of the 'fine ladies' saved women workers from being attracted to feminism and prevented any long or stable fraternization with bourgeois suffragettes.

The years 1905 and 1906 were marked by a particularly large number of women's meetings eagerly attended by women workers. The women workers listened carefully to the voice of the bourgeois suffragettes, but what was offered to them did not satisfy the urgent needs of those enslaved to capital, and did not evoke any whole-hearted response. The women of the working class were exhausted by the burden of intolerable working conditions, hunger and the material insecurity of their families; their immediate demands were: a shorter working day, higher pay, a more humane attitude on the part of the factory administration, less police surveillance, more freedom of action. All these demands were alien to bourgeois feminism. The suffragettes approached the women workers with narrowly feminine causes and aspirations. They did not and could not understand the class nature of the emerging women workers' movement. They were particularly disappointed by the domestic servants. On the initiative of the bourgeois feminists, the first meetings of domestic servants were held in St. Petersburg and Moscow in 1905. The domestic servants eagerly responded to this call to 'organize' and turned up at the early meetings in large numbers. However, when the Alliance for Female Equality tried to organize them to its own taste, i.e., to set up an idyllic, mixed alliance between lady employers and domestic employees, the domestic servants turned away from the suffragettes and, to the disappointment of the bourgeois ladies, 'hastened to join their own class party, organizing their own special trade unions'. Such is the state of affairs in Moscow, Vladimir, Penza, Kharkov and a number of other cities. The same fate befell attempts by another political women's organization even more to the right, the Women's Progressive Party, which attempted to organize domestic employees under the watchful eye of their mistresses. The domestic servants' movement overflowed the boundaries predetermined for it by the feminists. Look at the newspapers from 1905 and you will see that they abound in reports of direct action by domestic servants, even in the most remote regions of Russia. This action took the form either of mass strike action, or of street demonstrations. The strikes involved cooks, laundresses and maids; there were strikes according to profession, and strikes that united all 'domestic servants'. This protest by domestic employees spread like an infection from place to place. The demands made by the domestic servants were usually limited to an 8-hour working day, a minimum wage, more tolerable living conditions (a separate room), polite treatment by the employer, etc.

This political awakening of women was, moreover, not limited to the urban poor. For the first time in Russia, the Russian peasant woman also raised her voice persistently and resolutely. The end of 1904 and the whole of 1905 is a period of continuous 'petticoat rebellions', sparked off by the war against Japan. All the horrors and deprivations, all the social and economic ills that stemmed from this ill-fated war, weighed down on the peasant woman, wife and mother. The conscription of reserves placed a double burden of work and worry on her already overloaded shoulders, and forced her, hitherto dependent and fearful of everything that lay beyond the circle of her domestic interests, to meet face to face previously unsuspected hostile forces, and to become consciously aware of all her humiliation and deprivation, drain to the last drop the whole bitter cup of unmerited wrongs. . . . Illiterate, downtrodden peasant women left their homes and villages for the first time and hurried into town to wear down the steps of government offices in the attempt to obtain some news of their husbands, sons, and fathers, to petition for financial assistance and defend their interests. . . . The total lack of rights that was the peasant's lot, the lies and injustice of the existing social order, stood in all their naked ugliness before the bewildered peasant woman. . . . She returned from town sober and hardened, bearing in her heart an inexhaustible supply of bitterness, hatred and anger. . . . In the summer of 1905 a whole series of 'petticoat rebellions' broke out in the south. Filled with anger and with a boldness surprising for women, the peasant women attacked military and police headquarters where the army recruits were stationed, seized their menfolk and took them home. Armed with rakes, pitchforks and brooms, peasant women drove the armed guards from the villages. They are protesting in their own way against the intolerable burden of war. They are, of course, arrested, tried and given severe punishments, but the 'petticoat rebellions' continue. In this protest, defence of peasant interests and of purely 'female' interests are so closely interwoven that there are no grounds for dividing them and classing the 'petticoat rebellions' as part of the 'feminist movement'.

Following the 'political demonstrations' by the peasant women there come a series of 'petticoat rebellions' on economic grounds. This is the period of universal peasant unrest and agricultural strikes. The 'petticoats' sometimes initiated these disturbances, drawing the men after them. There were cases when, having failed to involve the men, the women marched to the manors by themselves to present their demands and ultimata. Arming themselves with whatever came to hand, they went ahead of the men to meet the punitive detachments. The downtrodden peasant woman, oppressed for centuries, suddenly became one of the central figures in the political drama. During the whole revolutionary period the peasant women, standing always united with their menfolk, guarded and defended peasant interests, and with amazing tact and sensitivity referred to their special, women's needs only when that did not endanger the common peasant cause.

This did not mean that the peasant women were indifferent to their needs as women, that they ignored them. On the contrary, the mass emergence of peasant women onto the political arena, their mass participation in the common struggle, reinforced and developed their feminine self-awareness. By November, 1905, the peasant women of the Voronezh province sent two of their own deputies to the peasant congress with instructions from the women's gathering to demand 'political rights' and 'freedom' for women on an equal basis with men.[1]

The female peasant population of the Caucasus defended their rights with particular vigour. The Guria peasant women at village meetings in the Kutaisi province adopted resolutions demanding political equality with men. At rural and urban meetings held to discuss the introduction of Zemstvos in Transcaucasia, the deputies representing the local population included Georgian women who insisted upon their rights as women.

While demanding political equality, the peasant women naturally always raised their voices in defence of their economic interests; the question of 'allotments' of land, concerned the peasant woman as much as it did the peasant man. In some

---

[1] It is sufficient to recall the historic written requests sent by the peasant women of the Voronezh and Tver provinces to the First State Duma, or the telegram sent by the peasant women from the village of Nogatkino to the deputy Aladyin:

'At this great moment in the battle between right and might, we, the peasant women of the village of Nogatkino, greet the elected delegates of the people who have expressed their lack of confidence in the government by demanding the resignation of the ministry. We hope that the representatives who have the support of the people will give that people land and freedom, will open the doors of the prisons and release those who fought for the freedom and happiness of the people, and that they will win civil and political rights both for themselves and for us, Russian women, who are without rights even in our own families. Remember that a woman slave cannot be the mother of a free citizen.' (Signed – the spokeswoman for 75 Nogatkino women.)

regions, peasant women who had enthusiastically supported the idea of expropriating private land, cooled in their support for this measure when the question arose as to whether the women would be included in the count to determine the size of the land allotment. 'If the land is taken from the landowners and given only to the men,' the women argued anxiously, 'then we will face real slavery. At present we can at least earn a few kopecks on our own account, whereas if that were to happen, we will simply be working for the men.' However, the fears of the peasant women proved to be completely unfounded; simple economic calculation obliged the peasantry to insist that land also be given to the women. The agrarian interests of the male and female sections of the peasantry were so closely interwoven that the men, in fighting to abolish the existing agricultural bondage for themselves, inevitably defended at the same time the economic interests of their womenfolk.

However, in fighting for the economic and political interests of the peasantry as a whole, the peasant woman also learned how to fight for her own specific needs and requirements as a woman. The same held true for the woman worker; with her unfailing participation in the whole liberation movement she, even more than the peasant woman, prepared public opinion to accept the principle of female equality. The idea of civic equality for women, now implemented in Soviet Russia, was spread through society not by the heroic efforts of individual women with forceful personalities, not by the struggle of the bourgeois feminists, but by the spontaneous pressure of broad masses of working and peasant women, who had been roused into life by the thunder of the first Russian revolution in 1905.

In 1909, in my book *The Social Basis of the Women's Question*, I said, arguing against the bourgeois feminists, against whom the whole of my book is directed: 'If the peasant woman does succeed in achieving in the near future an improvement in her domestic, economic and legal position, this will naturally be thanks only to the combined, united efforts of peasant democracy directed at obtaining the fulfillment of those peasant demands which, in one form or another, continue to be heard in the peasant milieu. Attempts by the feminists to 'clear the way for women', are here irrelevant. . . . If the peasant woman does free herself from the present agrarian bondage, she will receive more than all the feminist organizations put together could give her.'

These words, written ten years ago, have now been fully vindicated. The Great October Revolution has not only fulfilled the basic, urgent demand of the peasantry of both sexes that the land be transferred into the hands of those who work it, but has also raised the peasant woman to the honourable position of a free citizen equal in every respect, and now enslaved only by old methods of agricultural work and by still persisting family traditions and mores.

That of which the working and peasant women could only dream in the days of the first Russian revolution in 1905 has been translated into reality by the Great October Revolution of 1917.

Woman in Russia has achieved political equality. However she owes this achievement not to cooperation with bourgeois suffragettes, but to a joint, united struggle with her comrade workers in the ranks of her own working class.

# SEXUAL RELATIONS AND
# THE CLASS STRUGGLE
1921

Among the many problems that demand the consideration and attention of contemporary mankind, sexual problems are undoubtedly some of the most crucial. There isn't a country or a nation, apart from the legendary 'islands', where the question of sexual relationships isn't becoming an urgent and burning issue. Mankind today is living through an acute sexual crisis which is far more unhealthy and harmful for being long and drawn-out. Throughout the long journey of human history, you probably won't find a time when the problems of sex have occupied such a central place in the life of society; when the question of relationships between the sexes has been like a conjuror, attracting the attention of millions of troubled people; when sexual dramas have served as such a never-ending source of inspiration for every sort of art.

As the crisis continues and grows more serious, people are getting themselves into an increasingly hopeless situation, and are trying desperately by every available means to settle the 'insoluble question'. But with every new attempt to solve the problem, the confused knot of personal relationships gets more tangled. It's as if we couldn't see the one and only thread that could finally lead us to success in controlling the stubborn tangle. The sexual problem is like a vicious circle, and however frightened people are and however much they run this way and that, they are unable to break out.

The conservatively inclined part of mankind argue that we should return to the happy times of the past, we should re-establish the old foundations of the family and strengthen the well-tried norms of sexual morality. The champions of bourgeois individualism say that we ought to destroy all the hypocritical restrictions of the obsolete code of sexual behaviour. These unnecessary and repressive 'rags' ought to be relegated to the archives – only the individual conscience, the individual will of each person can decide such intimate questions. Socialists, on the other hand, assure us that sexual problems will only be settled when the basic reorganization of the social and economic structure of society has been tackled. Doesn't this 'putting off the problem until tomorrow' suggest that we still haven't found that one and only 'magic thread'? Shouldn't we find or at least locate this 'magic thread' that promises to unravel the tangle? Shouldn't we find it now, at this very moment? The history of human society, the history of the continual battle between various social groups and classes of opposing aims and interests, gives us the clue to finding this 'thread'. It isn't the first time that mankind has gone through a sexual crisis. This isn't the first time that the pressure of a rushing tide of new values and ideals has blurred the clear and definite meaning of moral commandments about sexual relationships. The 'sexual crisis' was particularly acute at the time of the Renaissance and the Reformation, when a great social advance pushed the proud and patriarchal feudal nobility who were used to absolute command into the background, and cleared the way for the development and establishment of a new social force – the bourgeoisie. The sexual morality of the feudal world had developed out of the depths of the tribal way of life the collective economy and the tribal authoritarian leadership that stifles the individual will of the individual member. This clashed with the new and strange moral code of the rising bourgeoisie. The sexual morality of the bourgeoisie is founded on principles that are in sharp contradiction to the basic morality of feudalism. Strict individualism and the exclusiveness and isolation of the 'nuclear family' replace the emphasis on collective work that was characteristic of both the local and regional economic structure of patrimonial life. Under capitalism the ethic of competition, the triumphant principles of individualism and exclusive private property, grew and destroyed whatever remained of the idea of the community, which was to some extent common to all types of tribal life. For a whole century, while the complex laboratory of life was turning the old norms into a new formula and achieving the outward harmony of moral ideas, men wandered confusedly between two very different sexual codes and attempted to accommodate themselves to both.

But in those bright and colourful days of change, the sexual crisis, although profound, did not have the threatening character that it has assumed in our time. The main reason for this is that in 'the great days' of the Renaissance, in the 'new age' when the bright light of a new spiritual culture flooded the dying world with its clear colours, flooded the bare monotonous life of the Middle Ages, the sexual crisis affected only a relatively small part of the population. By far the largest section of the population, the peasantry, was affected only in the most indirect way and only as, slowly, over the course of centuries, a change in the economic base, in the economic relations of the countryside, took place. At the top of the social ladder a bitter battle between two opposing social worlds was fought out. This involved also a struggle between their different ideals and values and ways of looking at things. It was these people who experienced and were threatened by the sexual crisis that developed. The peasants, wary of new things, continued to cling firmly to the well-tried tribal tradition handed down from their forefathers, and only under the pressure of extreme necessity modified and adapted this tradition to the changing conditions of their economic environment. Even at the height of the struggle between the bourgeois and the feudal world the sexual crisis by-passed the 'class of tax-payers'. As the upper strata of society went about breaking up the old ways, the peasants in fact seemed to be more intent on clinging firmly to their traditions. In spite of the continuous whirlwinds that threatened overhead and shook the very soil under their feet, the peasants, especially our Russian peasantry, managed to preserve the basis of their sexual code untouched and unshaken for many centuries.

The story today is very different. The 'sexual crisis' does not spare even the peasantry. Like an infectious disease it 'knows neither mansions to the rank nor status'. It spreads from the palaces and crowded quarters of the working class, looks in on the peaceful dwelling places of the petty bourgeoisie, and makes its way into the heart of the countryside. It claims victims in the villas of the European bourgeoisie, in the fusty basement of the worker's family, and in the smoky hut of the peasant. There is 'no defence, no bolt' against sexual conflict. To imagine that only the members of the well-off sections of society are floundering and are in the throes of these problems would be to make a grave mistake. The waves of the sexual crisis are sweeping over the threshold of workers' homes, and creating situations of conflict that are as acute and heartfelt as the psychological sufferings of the 'refined bourgeois world'. The sexual crisis no longer interests only the 'propertied'. The problems of sex concern the largest section of society they – concern the working class in its daily life. It is, therefore, hard to understand why this vital and urgent subject is treated with such indifference. This indifference is unforgivable. One of the tasks that confront the working class in its attack on the 'beleaguered fortress of the future' is undoubtedly the task of establishing more healthy and more joyful relationships between the sexes.

What are the roots of this unforgivable indifference to one of the essential tasks of the working class? How can we explain to ourselves the hypocritical way in which 'sexual problems' are relegated to the realm of 'private matters' that are not worth the effort and attention of the collective? Why has the fact been ignored that throughout history one of the constant features of social struggle has been the attempt to change relationships between the sexes, and the type of moral codes that determine these relationships; and that the way personal relationships are organized in a certain social group has had a vital influence on the outcome of the struggle between hostile social classes?

The tragedy of our society is not just that the usual forms of behaviour and the principles regulating this behaviour are breaking down, but that a spontaneous wave of new attempts at living is developing from within the social fabric, giving man hopes and ideals that cannot yet be realized. We are people living in the world of property relationships, a world of sharp class contradictions and of an individualistic morality. We still live and think under the heavy hand of an unavoidable loneliness of spirit. Man experiences this 'loneliness' even in towns full of shouting, noise and people, even in a crowd of close friends and work-mates. Because of their loneliness men are apt to cling in a predatory and unhealthy way to illusions about finding a 'soul mate' from among the members of the opposite sex. They see sly Eros as the only means of charming away, if only for a time, the gloom of inescapable loneliness.

People have perhaps never in any age felt spiritual loneliness as deeply and persistently as at the present time. People have probably never become so depressed and fallen so fully under the numbing influence of this loneliness. It could hardly be otherwise. The darkness never seems so black as when there's a light shining just ahead.

The 'individualists', who are only loosely organized into a collective with other individuals, now have the chance to change their sexual relationships so that they are based on the creative principle of friendship and togetherness rather than on something blindly physiological. The individualistic property morality of the present day is beginning to seem very obviously paralysing and oppressive. In criticizing the quality of sexual relationships modern man is doing far more than rejecting the outdated forms of behaviour of the current moral code. His lonely soul is seeking the regeneration of the very essence of these relationships. He moans and pines for 'great love', for a situation of warmth and creativity which alone has the power to disperse the cold spirit of loneliness from which present day 'individualists' suffer.

If the sexual crisis is three quarters the result of external socioeconomic relationships, the other quarter hinges on our 'refined individualistic psyche', fostered by the ruling bourgeois ideology. The 'potential for loving' of people today is, as the German writer Meisel-Hess puts it, at a low ebb. Men and women seek each other in the hope of finding for themselves, through another person, a means to a larger share of spiritual and physical pleasure. It makes no difference whether they are married to the partner or not, they give little thought to what's going on in the other person, to what's happening to their emotions and psychological processes.

The 'crude individualism' that adorns our era is perhaps nowhere as blatant as in the organization of sexual relationships. A person wants to escape from his loneliness and naively imagines that being 'in love' gives him the right to the soul of the other person – the right to warm himself in the rays of that rare blessing of emotional closeness and understanding. We individualists have had our emotions spoiled in the persistent cult of the 'ego'. We imagine that we can reach the happiness of being in a state of 'great love' with those near to us, without having to 'give up' anything of ourselves.

The claims we make on our 'contracted partner' are absolute and undivided. We are unable to follow the simplest rule of love – that another person should be treated with great consideration. New concepts of the relationships between the sexes are already being outlined. They will teach us to achieve relationships based on the unfamiliar ideas of complete freedom, equality and genuine friendship. But in the meantime mankind has to sit in the cold with its spiritual loneliness and can only dream about the 'better age' when all relationships between people will be warmed by the rays of 'the sun god', will experience a sense of togetherness, and will be educated in the new conditions of living. The sexual crisis cannot be solved unless there is a radical reform of the human psyche, and unless man's potential for loving is increased. And a basic transformation of the socio-economic relationships along communist lines is, essential if the psyche is to be re-formed. This is an 'old truth' but there is no other way out. The sexual crisis will in no way be reduced, whatever kind of marriage or personal relationships people care to try.

History has never seen such a variety of personal relationships – indissoluble marriage with its 'stable family', 'free unions', secret adultery; a girl living quite openly with her lover in so-called 'wild marriage'; pair marriage, marriage in threes and even the complicated marriage of four people – not to talk of the various forms of commercial prostitution. You get the same two moral codes existing side by side in the peasantry as well – a mixture of the old tribal way of life and the developing bourgeois family. Thus you get the permissiveness of the girls' house,[1] side by side with the attitude that fornication, or men sleeping with their daughters-in-law, is a disgrace. It's surprising that in the face of the contradictory and tangled forms of present-day personal relationships, people are able to preserve a faith in moral authority, and are able to make sense of these contradictions and thread their way through these mutually destructive and incompatible moral codes. Even the usual justification – 'I live by the new morality' – doesn't help anyone, since the new morality is still only in the process of being formed. Our task is to draw out from the chaos of present-day contradictory sexual norms the shape, and make clear the principles, of a morality that answers the spirit of the progressive and revolutionary class.

Besides the already mentioned inadequacies of the contemporary psyche – extreme individuality, egoism that has become a cult – the 'sexual crisis' is made worse by two characteristics of the psychology of modern man:

1. The idea of 'possessing' the married partner;
2. The belief that the two sexes are unequal, that they are of unequal worth in every way, in every sphere, including the sexual sphere.

[1] In the traditional Russian villages, the young girls would often get together to rent an old hut or a room in someone's house. They would gather there in the evenings to tell stories, do needlework and sing. The young men would come to join in the merrymaking. Sometimes it seems that the merrymaking would become an orgy, though there are conflicting ideas about this.

Bourgeois morality, with its introverted individualistic family based entirely on private property, has carefully cultivated the idea that one partner should completely 'possess' the other. It has been very successful. The idea of 'possession' is more pervasive now than under the patrimonial system of marriage relationships. During the long historical period that developed under the aegis of the 'tribe', the idea of a man possessing his wife (there has never been any thought of a wife having undisputed possession of her husband) did not go further than a purely physical possession. The wife was obliged to be faithful physically – her soul was her own. Even the knights recognized the right of their wives to have *chichesbi* (platonic friends and admirers) and to receive the 'devotion' of other knights and minnesingers. It is the bourgeoisie who have carefully tended and fostered the ideal of absolute possession of the 'contracted partner's' emotional as well as physical 'I', thus extending the concept of property rights to include the right to the other person's whole spiritual and emotional world. Thus the family structure was strengthened and stability guaranteed in the period when the bourgeoisie were struggling for domination. This is the ideal that we have accepted as our heritage and have been prepared to see as an unchangeable moral absolute! The idea of 'property' goes far beyond the boundaries of 'lawful marriage'. It makes itself felt as an inevitable ingredient of the most 'free' union of love. Contemporary lovers with all their respect for freedom are not satisfied by the knowledge of the physical faithfulness alone of the person they love. To be rid of the eternally present threat of loneliness, we 'launch an attack' on the emotions of the person we love with a cruelty and lack of delicacy that will not he understood by future generations. We demand the right to know every secret of this person's being. The modern lover would forgive physical unfaithfulness sooner than 'spiritual' unfaithfulness. He sees any emotion experienced outside the boundaries of the 'free' relationship as the loss of his own personal treasure.

People 'in love' are unbelievably insensitive in their relations to a third person. We have all no doubt observed this strange situation: two people who love each other are in a hurry, before they have got to know each other properly, to exercise their rights over all the relationships that the other person has formed up till that time, to look into the innermost corners of their partner's life. Two people who yesterday were unknown to each other, and who come together in a single moment of mutual erotic feeling, rush to get at the heart of the other person's being. They want to feel that this strange and incomprehensible psyche, with its past experience that can never be suppressed, is an extension of their own self. The idea that the married pair are each other's property is so accepted that when a young couple who were yesterday each living their own separate lives are today opening each other's correspondence without a blush, and making common property of the words of a third person who is a friend of only one of them, this hardly strikes us as something unnatural. But this kind of 'intimacy' is only really possible when people have been working out their lives together for a long period of time. Usually a dishonest kind of closeness is substituted for this genuine feeling, the deception being fostered by the mistaken idea that a physical relationship between two people is a sufficient basis for extending the rights of possession to each other's emotional being.

The 'inequality' of the sexes – the inequality of their rights, the unequal value of their physical and emotional experience – is the other significant circumstance that distorts the psyche of contemporary man and is a reason for the deepening of the 'sexual crisis'. The 'double morality' inherent in both patrimonial and bourgeois society has, over the course of centuries, poisoned the psyche of men and women. These attitudes are so much a part of us that they are more difficult to get rid of than the ideas about possessing people that we have inherited only from bourgeois ideology. The idea that the sexes are unequal, even in the sphere of physical and emotional experience, means that the same action will be regarded differently according to whether it was the action of a man or a woman. Even the most 'progressive' member of the bourgeoisie, who has long ago rejected the whole code of current morality, easily catches himself out at this point since he too in judging a man and a woman for the same behaviour will pass different sentences. One simple example is enough. Imagine that a member of the middle-class intelligentsia who is learned, involved in politics and social affairs – who is in short a 'personality', even a 'public figure' – starts sleeping with his cook (a not uncommon thing to happen) and even becomes legally married to her. Does bourgeois society change its attitude to this man, does the event throw even the tiniest shadow of doubt as to his moral worth? Of course not.

Now imagine another situation. A respected woman of bourgeois society – a social figure, a research student, a doctor, or a writer, it's all the same – becomes friendly with her footman, and to complete the scandal marries him. How does bourgeois society react to the behaviour of the hitherto 'respected' woman? They cover her with 'scorn', of course! And remember, it's so much the worse for her if her husband, the footman, is good-looking or possesses other 'physical qualities'. 'It's obvious what she's fallen for,' will be the sneer of the hypocritical bourgeoisie.

If a woman's choice has anything of an 'individual character' about it she won't be forgiven by bourgeois society. This attitude is a kind of throwback to the traditions of tribal times. Society still wants a woman to take into account, when she is making her choice, rank and status and the instructions and interests of her family. Bourgeois society cannot see a woman as an independent person separate from her family unit and outside the isolated circle of domestic obligations and virtues. Contemporary society goes even further than the ancient tribal society in acting as woman's trustee, instructing her not only to marry but to fall in love only with those people who are 'worthy' of her.

We are continually meeting men of considerable spiritual and intellectual qualities who have chosen as their friend-for-life a

**101**

worthless and empty woman, who in no way matches the spiritual worth of the husband. We accept this as something normal and we don't think twice about it. At the most friends might pity Ivan Ivanovich for having landed himself with such an unbearable wife. But if it happens the other way round, we flap our hands and exclaim with concern. 'How could such an outstanding woman as Maria Petrovna fall for such a nonentity? I begin to doubt the worth of Maria Petrovna.' Where do we get this double criterion from? What is the reason for it? The reason is undoubtedly that the idea of the sexes being of 'different value' has become, over the centuries, a part of man's psychological make-up. We are used to evaluating a woman not as a personality with individual qualities and failings irrespective of her physical and emotional experience, but only as an appendage of a man. This man, the husband or the lover, throws the light of his personality over the woman, and it is this reflection and not the woman herself that we consider to be the true definition of her emotional and moral make-up. In the eyes of society the personality of a man can be more easily separated from his actions in the sexual sphere. The personality of a woman is judged almost exclusively in terms of her sexual life. This type of attitude stems from the role that women have played in society over the centuries, and it is only now that a re-evaluation of these attitudes is slowly being achieved, at least in outline. Only a change in the economic role of woman, and her independent involvement in production, can and will bring about the weakening of these mistaken and hypocritical ideas.

The three basic circumstances distorting the modern psyche – extreme egoism, the idea that married partners possess each other, and the acceptance of the inequality of the sexes in terms of physical and emotional experience – must be faced if the sexual problem is to be settled. People will find the 'magic key' with which they can break out of their situation only when their psyche has a sufficient store of 'feelings of consideration', when their ability to love is greater, when the idea of freedom in personal relationships becomes fact and when the principle of 'comradeship' triumphs over the traditional idea of 'inequality' and submission. The sexual problems cannot be solved without this radical re-education of our psyche.

But isn't this asking too much? Isn't the suggestion utopian without foundation, the naive notion of a dreaming idealist? How are you honestly going to raise mankind's 'potential for loving'? Haven't wise men of all nations since time immemorial, beginning with Buddha and Confucius and ending with Christ, been busying themselves over this? And who can say if the – 'potential for loving' has been raised? Isn't this a kind of well-meaning daydream about the solution of the sexual crisis simply a confession of weakness and a refusal to go on with the search for the 'magic key'?

Is that the case? Is the radical re-education of our psyche and our approach to sexual relationships something so unlikely, so removed from reality? Couldn't one say that, on the contrary, while great social and economic changes are in progress, the conditions are being created that demand and give rise to a new basis for psychological experience that is in line with what we have been talking about? Another class, a new social group, is coming forward to replace the bourgeoisie, with its bourgeois ideology, and its individualistic code of sexual morality. The progressive class, as it develops in strength, cannot fail to reveal new ideas about relationships between the sexes that form in close connection with the problems of its social class.

The complicated evolution of socio-economic relations taking place before our eyes, which changes all our ideas about the role of women in social life and undermines the sexual morality of the bourgeoisie, has two contradictory results. On the one hand we see mankind's tireless efforts to adapt to the new, changing socio-economic conditions. This is manifest either in an attempt to preserve the 'old forms' while providing them with a new content (the observance of the external form of the indissoluble, strictly monogamous marriage with an acceptance, in practice, of the freedom of the partners) or in the acceptance of new forms which contain however all the elements of the moral code of bourgeois marriage (the 'free' union where the compulsive possessiveness of the partners is greater than within legal marriage). On the other hand we see the slow but steady appearance of new forms of relationships between the sexes that differ from the old norms in outward form and in spirit.

Mankind is not groping its way toward these new ideas with much confidence, but we need to look at its attempt, however vague it is at the moment, since it is an attempt closely linked with the tasks of the proletariat as the class which is to capture the 'beleaguered fortress' of the future. If, amongst the complicated labyrinth of contradictory and tangled sexual norms, you want to find the beginnings of more healthy relationships between the sexes – relationships that promise to lead humanity out of the sexual crisis – you have to leave the 'cultured quarters' of the bourgeoisie with their refined individualistic psyche, and take a look at the huddled dwelling-places of the working class. There, amidst the horror and squalor of capitalism, amidst tears and curses, the springs of life are welling up.

You can see the double process which we have just mentioned working itself out in the lives of the proletariat, who have to exist under the pressure of harsh economic conditions, cruelly exploited by capitalism. You can see both the process of 'passive adjustment' and that of active opposition to the existing reality. The destructive influence of capitalism destroys the basis of the worker's family and forces him unconsciously to 'adapt' to the existing conditions. This gives rise to a whole series of situations with regard to relationships between the sexes similar to those in other social classes. Under the pressure of low wages the worker inevitably tends to get married at a later age. If twenty years ago a worker usually got married between the ages of twenty and twenty-five, he now shoulders the cares of a family only towards his thirtieth year. The higher the cultural demands of the worker – the more he values the opportunity of being in contact with cultural life, of visiting theatres and lectures, of reading papers and magazines, of giving his spare time to struggle and politics or to some favourite pursuit such as art or reading, etc. – the later he tends to get married. But physical needs won't take a financial situation into consideration: they insist on making themselves felt. The working-class bachelor, in the same way as the middle-class bachelor, looks to prostitution for an outlet. This is an example of the passive adjustment of the working class to the unfavourable conditions of their existence. Take another example – when the worker marries, the low level of pay forces the worker's family to 'regulate' childbirth just as the bourgeois family does. The frequent cases of infanticide, the growth of prostitution – these are all expressions of the same process. These are all examples of adjustment by the working class to the surrounding reality. But this is not a process characteristic of the proletariat alone. All the other classes and sections of the population caught up in the world process of capitalist development react in this way.

We see a difference only when we begin to talk about the active, creative forces at work that oppose rather than adapt to the repressive reality, and about the new ideals and attempts at new relationship between the sexes. It is only within the working class that this active opposition is taking shape. This doesn't mean that the other classes and sections of the population (particularly the middle-class intelligentsia who, by the circumstances of their social existence, stand closest to the working class) don't adopt the 'new' forms that are being worked out by the progressive working class. The bourgeoisie, motivated by an instinctive desire to breathe new life into their dead and feeble forms of marriage, seize upon the 'new' ideas of the working class. But the ideals and code of sexual morality that the working class develops do not reflect the class needs of the bourgeoisie. They reflect the demands of the working class and therefore serve as a new weapon in its social struggle. They help shatter the foundations of the social domination of the bourgeoisie. Let us make this point clear by an example.

The attempt by the middle-class intelligentsia to replace indissoluble marriage by the freer, more easily broken ties of civil marriage destroys the essential basis of the social stability of the bourgeoisie. It destroys the monogamous, property-orientated family. On the other hand, a greater fluidity in relationships between the sexes coincides with and is even the indirect result of one of the basic tasks of the working class. The rejection of the element of 'submission' in marriage is going to destroy the last artificial ties of the bourgeois family. This act of 'submission' on the part of one member of the working class to another, in the same way as the sense of possessiveness in relationships, has a harmful effect on the proletarian psyche. It is not in the interests of that revolutionary class to elect only certain members as its independent representatives, whose duty it is to serve the class interests before the interests of the individual, isolated family. Conflicts between the interests of the family and the interests of the class which occur at the time of a strike or during an active struggle, and the moral yardstick with which the proletariat views such events, are sufficiently clear evidence of the basis of the new proletarian ideology.

Suppose family affairs require a businessman to take his capital out of a firm at a time when the enterprise is in financial difficulties. Bourgeois morality is clear-cut in its estimate of his action: 'The interests of the family come first.' We can compare with this the attitude of workers to a strikebreaker who defies his comrades and goes to work during a strike to save his family from being hungry. 'The interests of the class come first.' Here's another example. The love and loyalty of the middle-class husband to his family are sufficient to divert his wife from all interests outside the home and end up by tying her to the nursery and the kitchen. 'The ideal husband can support the ideal family' is the way the bourgeoisie looks at it. But how do workers look upon a 'conscious' member of their class who shuts the eyes of his wife or girl-friend to the social struggle? For the sake of individual happiness, for the sake of the family, the morality of the working class will demand that women take part in the life that is unfolding beyond the doorsteps. The 'captivity' of women in the home, the way family interests are placed before all else, the widespread exercise of absolute property rights by the husband over the wife – all these things are being broken down by the basic principle of the working-class ideology of 'comradely solidarity'. The idea that some members are unequal and must submit to other members of one and the same class is in contradiction with the basic proletarian principle of comradeship. This principle of comradeship is basic to the ideology of the working class. It colours and determines the whole developing proletarian morality, a morality which helps to re-educate the personality of man, allowing him to be capable of feeling, capable of freedom instead of being bound by a sense of property, capable of comradeship rather than inequality and submission.

It is an old truth that every new class that develops as a result an advance in economic growth and material culture offers mankind an appropriately new ideology. The code of sexual behaviour is a part of this ideology. However it is worth saying something about 'proletarian ethics' or 'proletarian sexual morality', in order to criticize the well-worn idea that proletarian sexual morality is no more than 'super-structure' and that there is no place for any change in this sphere until the economic base of society has been changed. As if the ideology of a certain class is formed only when the breakdown in the socio-economic relationships, guaranteeing the dominance of that class, has been completed! All the experience of history teaches us that a social group works out its ideology, and consequently its sexual morality, in the process of its struggle with hostile social forces.

Only with the help of new spiritual values, created within and answering the needs of the class, will that class manage to strengthen its social position. It can only successfully win power from those groups in society that are hostile to it by holding to these new norms and ideals. To search for the basic criteria for a morality that can reflect the interests of the working class, and to see that the developing sexual norms are in accordance with these criteria – this is the task that *must* be tackled by the ideologists of the working class. We have to understand that it is only by becoming aware of the creative process that *is going* on within society, and of the new demands, new ideals and new norms that are being formed, only by becoming clear about the bash of the sexual morality of the progressive class, that we can possibly make sense of the chaos and contradictions of sexual relationships and find the thread that will make it possible to undo the tightly rolled up tangle of sexual problems.

We must remember that only a code of sexual morality that is in harmony with the problems of the working class can serve as an important weapon in strengthening the working class' fighting position. The experience of history teaches us that much. What can stop us using this weapon in the interests of the working class, who are fighting for a communist system and for new relationships between the sexes that are deeper and more joyful?

# THESES ON COMMUNIST MORALITY
# IN THE SPHERE OF MARITAL RELATIONS
## 1921

Family and marriage are historical categories, phenomena which develop in accordance with the economic relations that exist at the given level of production. The form of marriage and of the family is thus determined by the economic system of the given epoch, and it changes as the economic base of society changes. The family, in the same way as government, religion, science, morals, law and customs, is part of the superstructure which derives from the economic system of society.

Where economic functions are performed by the family rather than by society as a whole, family and marital relations are more stable and possess a vital capacity: 'The less the development of labour, and the more limited its volume of production . . . the more preponderantly does the social order appear to be dominated by ties of sex' (Engels, *Origins of the Family*). In the period of natural economy the family formed an enclosed economic unit which was necessary for humankind and thus had a vital capacity. The family was at that time a unit of both production and consumption. Outside the family/economic unit the individual had no means, especially at the earliest levels of the development of society, of sustaining the conditions necessary for life. In some areas and in some countries where capitalism is weakly developed (among the peoples of the East, for example) the peasant family is still fundamentally a family/economic union. With the transition, however, from a natural economy to a merchant capitalist economy based on trade and exchange, the family ceases to be necessary for the functioning of society and thus loses its strength and vital capacity.

The fact that with the consolidation of the capitalist system of production, the marital/family union develops from a production unit into a legal arrangement concerned only with consumption, leads inevitably to the weakening of marital/family ties. In the era of private property and the bourgeois-capitalist economic system, marriage and the family are grounded in (a) material and financial considerations, (b) economic dependence of the female sex on the family breadwinner – the husband – rather than the social collective, and (c) the need to care for the rising generation. Capitalism maintains a system of individual economies: the family has a role to play in performing economic tasks and functions within the national capitalist economy. Thus under capitalism the family does not merge with or dissolve into the national economy but continues to exist as an independent economic unit, concerned with production in the case of the peasant family and consumption in the case of the urban family. The individual economy which springs from private property is the basis of the bourgeois family.

The communist economy does away with the family. In the period of the dictatorship of the proletariat there is a transition to the single production plan and collective social consumption, and the family loses its significance as an economic unit. The external economic functions of the family disappear, and consumption ceases to be organized on an individual family basis, a network of social kitchens and canteens is established, and the making, mending and washing of clothes and other aspects of housework 'are integrated into the national economy'. In the period of the dictatorship of the proletariat the family economic unit should be recognized as being, from the point of view of the national economy, not only useless but harmful. The family economic unit involves (a) the uneconomic expenditure of products and fuel on the part of small domestic economies, and (b) unproductive labour, especially by women, in the home – and is therefore in conflict with the interest of the workers' republic in a single economic plan and the expedient use of the labour force (including women).

Under the dictatorship of the proletariat then, the material and economic considerations in which the family was grounded cease to exist. The economic dependence of women on men and the role of the family in the care of 'the younger generation' also disappear as the communist elements in the workers' republic grow stronger. With the introduction of the obligation of all citizens to work, woman has a value in the national economy which is independent of her family and marital status. The economic subjugation of women in marriage and the family is done away with, and responsibility for the care of the children and their physical and spiritual education is assumed by the social collective. The family teaches and instills egoism thus weakening the ties of the collective and hindering the construction of communism. However, in the new society relations between parents and children are freed from any element of material considerations and enter a new historic stage.

Once the family has been stripped of its economic functions and its responsibilities towards the younger generation and is no longer central to the existence of the woman, it has ceased to be a family. The family unit shrinks to a union of two people based on mutual agreement.

In the period of the dictatorship of the proletariat, the workers' state has to concern itself not with the economic and social unit of the family, since this unit dies as the bonds of communism are consolidated, but with the changing forms of marital relations. The family as an economic unit and as a union of parents and children based on the need to provide for the material welfare of the latter is doomed to disappear. Thus the workers' collective has to establish its attitude not to economic relationships but to the form of relationships between the sexes. What kind of relations between the sexes are in the best interests of the workers' collective? What form of relations would strengthen, not weaken, the collective in the transitional stage between capitalism and communism and would thus assist the construction of the new society? The laws and the morality that the workers' system is evolving are beginning to give an answer to this question.

Once relations between the sexes cease to perform the economic and social function of the former family, they are no longer the concern of the workers' collective. It is not the relationships between the sexes but the result – the child – that concerns the collective. The workers' state recognizes its responsibility to provide for maternity, i.e., to guarantee the well-being of the woman and the child, but it does not recognize the couple as a legal unit separate from the workers' collective. The decrees on marriage issued by the workers' republic establishing the mutual rights of the married couple (the right to demand material support from the partner for yourself or the child), and thus giving legal encouragement to the separation of this unit and its interests from the general interests of the workers' social collective (the right of wives to be transferred to the town or village where their husbands are working), are survivals of the past; they contradict the interests of the collective and weaken its bonds, and should therefore be reviewed and changed.

The law ought to emphasize the interest of the workers' collective in maternity and eliminate the situation where the child is dependent on the relationship between its parents. The law of the workers' collective replaces the right of the parents, and the workers' collective keeps a close watch, in the interests of the unified economy and of present and future labour resources. In the period of the dictatorship of the proletariat there must, instead of marriage law, be regulation of the relationship of the government to maternity, of the relationship between mother and child and of the relationship between the mother and the workers' collective (i.e., legal norms must regulate the protection of female labour, the welfare of expectant and nursing mothers, the welfare of children and their social education). Legal norms must regulate the relationship between the mother and the socially educated child, and between the father and the child. Fatherhood should not be established through marriage or a relationship of a material nature. The man should be able to choose whether or not to accept the role of fatherhood (i.e., the right which he shares equally with the mother to decide on a social system of education for the child, and the right, where this does not conflict with the interests of the collective, of intellectual contact with the child and the opportunity to influence its development).

There are two grounds on which, in the interests of the workers' collective, the relationships between the sexes ought to be subject to legislative regulations: (a) the health and hygiene of the nation and the race, and (b) the increase or decrease of the population required by the national economic collective. In the period of the dictatorship of the proletariat, the regulation of relationships enters a new phase. Instead of laws and the threat of legal proceedings, the workers' collective must rely on agitational and educational influences, and on social measures to improve the relationships between the sexes and to guarantee the health of the children born from these relationships. For example, the Commissariats of Health and Education must carry out a broad campaign on the question of venereal and other infectious diseases, thereby reducing the danger of these diseases spreading through sexual intercourse and daily living. A person is guilty before the law not for having had sexual relations but for having consciously kept silent and hidden the fact that he or she has the disease from those with whom he or she lives and works, and thus for failing to observe the rule on precautions to be taken to reduce the likelihood of infection.

In the period of the dictatorship of the proletariat, communist Morality – and not the law – regulates sexual relationships in the interest of the workers' collective and of future generations.

Each historical (and therefore economic) epoch in the development of society has its own ideal of marriage and its own sexual morality. Under the tribal system, with its ties of kinship, the morality was different from that which developed with the establishment of private property and the rule of the husband and father (patriarchy). Different economic systems have different moral codes. Not only each stage in the development of society, but each class has its corresponding sexual morality (it is sufficient to compare the morals of the feudal landowning class and of the bourgeoisie in one and the same epoch to see that this is true). The more firmly established the principles of private property, the stricter the moral code. The importance of virginity before legal marriage sprang from the principles of private property and the unwillingness of men to pay for the children of others.

Hypocrisy (the outward observance of decorum and the actual practice of depravity), and the double code (one code of behaviour for the man and another for the woman) are the twin pillars of bourgeois morality. Communist morality must above all, resolutely spurn all the hypocrisy inherited from bourgeois society in relationships between the sexes, and reject the double standard of morality.

In the period of the dictatorship of the proletariat relations between the sexes should be evaluated only according to the criteria mentioned above – the health of the working population and the development of inner bonds of solidarity within the collective. The sexual act must be seen not as something shameful and sinful but as something which is as natural as the other needs of a healthy organism, such as hunger and thirst. Such phenomena cannot be judged as moral or immoral. The satisfaction of healthy and natural instincts only ceases to be normal when the boundaries of hygiene are overstepped. In such cases, not only the health of the person concerned but the interests of the work collective, which needs the strength and energy and health of its members, are threatened. Communist morality, therefore, while openly recognizing the normality of sexual interests, condemns unhealthy and unnatural interest in sex (excesses, for example, or sexual relations before maturity has been reached, which exhaust the organism and lower the capacity of men and women for work).

As communist morality is concerned for the health of the population, it also criticizes sexual restraint. The preservation of health includes the full and correct satisfaction of all man's needs; norms of hygiene should work to this end, and not artificially suppress such an important function of the organism as the sex drive (Bebel, *Woman and Socialism*). Thus both early sexual experience (before the body has developed and grown strong) and sexual restraint must be seen as equally harmful. This concern for the health of the human race does not establish either monogamy or polygamy as the obligatory form of relations between the sexes, for excesses may be committed in the bounds of the former, and a frequent change of partners by no means signifies sexual intemperance. Science has discovered that when a woman has relationships with many men at one time, her ability to have children is impaired; and relationships with a number of women drain the man and affect the health of his children negatively. Since the workers' collective needs strong and healthy men and women, such arrangements of sexual life are not in its interests.

It is accepted that the psychological state of parents at the moment of conception influences the health and life capacity of the child. Thus in the interests of human health, communist morality criticizes sexual relations which are based on physical attraction alone and are not attended to by love or fleeting passion. In the interests of the collective, communist morality also criticizes persons whose sexual relationships are built not on physical attraction but on calculation, habit or even intellectual affinity.

In view of the need to encourage the development and growth of feelings of solidarity and to strengthen the bonds of the work collective, it should above all be established that the isolation of the 'couple' as a special unit does not answer the interests of communism. Communist morality requires the education of the working class in comradeship and the fusion of the hearts and minds of the separate members of this collective. The needs and interests of the individual must be subordinated to the interests and aims of the collective. On the one hand, therefore, the bonds of family and marriage must be weakened, and on the other, men and women need to be educated in solidarity and the subordination of the will of the individual to the will of the collective. Even at this present, early stage, the workers' republic demands that mothers learn to be the mothers not only of their own child but of all workers' children; it does not recognize the couple as a self-sufficient unit, and does not therefore approve of wives deserting work for the sake of this unit.

As regards sexual relations, communist morality demands first of all an end to all relations based on financial or other economic considerations. The buying and selling of caresses destroys the sense of equality between the sexes, and thus undermines the basis of solidarity without which communist society cannot exist. Moral censure is consequently directed at prostitution in all its forms and at all types of marriage of convenience, even when recognized by Soviet law. The preservation of marriage regulations creates the illusion that the workers' collective can accept the 'couple' with its special, exclusive interests. The stronger the ties between the members of the collective, as a whole, the less the need to reinforce marital relations. Secondly, communist morality demands the education of the younger generation in responsibility to the collective and in the consciousness that love is not the only thing in life (this is especially important in the case of women, for they have been taught the opposite for centuries). Love is only one aspect of life, and must not be allowed to overshadow the other facets of the relationships between individual and collective. The ideal of the bourgeoisie was the married couple, where the partners complemented each other so completely that they had no need of contact with society. Communist morality demands, on the contrary, that the younger generation be educated in such a way that the personality of the individual is developed to the full, and the individual with his or her many interests has contact with a range of persons of both sexes. Communist morality encourages the development of many and varied bonds of love and friendship among people. The old ideal was 'all for the loved ones'; communist morality demands all for the collective.

Though sex love is seen in the context of the interests of the collective, communist morality demands that people are educated in sensitivity and understanding and are psychologically demanding both to themselves and to their partners. The bourgeois attitude to sexual relations as simply a matter of sex must be criticized and replaced by an understanding of the whole gamut of joyful love-experience that enriches life and makes for greater happiness. The greater the intellectual and emotional development of the individual the less place will there be in his or her relationship for the bare physiological side of love, and the brighter will be the love experience.

In the transitional period, relations between men and women must, in order to meet the interests of the workers' collective, he based on the following considerations. (1) All sexual relationships must be based on mutual inclination, love, infatuation or passion, and in no case on financial or material motivations. All calculation in relationships must be subject to merciless condemnation. (2) The form and length of the relationship are not regulated, but the hygiene of the race, and communist morality require that relationships be based not on the sexual act alone, and that it should not be accompanied by any excesses that threaten health. (3) Those with illnesses etc. that might be inherited should not have children. (4) A jealous and proprietary attitude to the person loved must be replaced by a comradely understanding of the other and an acceptance of his or her freedom. Jealousy is a destructive force of which communist morality cannot approve. (5) The bonds between the members of the collective must be strengthened. The encouragement of the intellectual, and political interests of the younger generation assists the development of healthy and bright emotions in love.

The stronger the collective, the more firmly established becomes the communist way of life. The closer the emotional ties between the members of the community, the less the need to seek a refuge from loneliness in marriage. Under communism the blind strength of matter is subjugated to the will of the strongly welded and thus unprecedentedly powerful workers' collective. The individual has the opportunity to develop intellectually and emotionally as never before, in this collective, new forms of relationships are maturing and the concept of love is extended and expanded.

## WHAT HAS THE OCTOBER REVOLUTION DONE FOR WOMEN IN THE WEST?
1927

What the October Revolution has achieved in terms of the emancipation of working women in the Soviet Union is well known to all, is clear and indisputable. However, what effect has the Great October Revolution had on the movement for the emancipation of women in other, bourgeois countries abroad? What has it contributed to the creation of the 'new woman' involved in the tasks and aspirations of the working class?

World war, which, in Europe and North America, *drew* enormous numbers of women from the poorer sections of the population, and those with *moderate means* into the whirlpool of production and state administration, undoubtedly served to advance considerably the cause of female emancipation. The rapid growth of female labour brought with it unparalleled changes in family life, and in the overall mode of life of women in bourgeois countries. However, this process of female emancipation would scarcely have advanced any further, without the powerful example of the October Revolution. The October Revolution helped to bring about a new evaluation of women, to reveal and confirm the view of women as socially useful labour units. From the very first days of the October Revolution it became clear that women's energies are needed not only by the husband and the family, as had been thought for thousands of years, but also by society, the whole social collective, the state.

However, that this phenomenon is an inevitable historical fact, that the formation of a new type of woman is linked to a general shift towards the creation of a new, working society, is something that the bourgeoisie cannot and does not wish to recognize. If it were not for the October Revolution, it would still be generally believed that the woman earning her own living is a temporary phenomenon, and that the woman's place is in the family, standing at the back of her husband bread-winner. The October Revolution changed many concepts. This radical change in the evaluation of the tasks and vocation of women in the Soviet Union has affected the attitude to women far beyond the borders of the Soviet Union. We can now meet the new woman everywhere, in every corner of the world. The new woman is a mass phenomenon, with the exception, perhaps, of women in the semi-colonial and colonial countries, where the development of the productive forces is impeded by the predatory rule of the imperialists. However, even there, given the struggle for national self-determination and against imperialism, the new woman is being moulded in the very process of struggle. It is impossible to succeed in the struggle between social groups and classes without the cooperation of women.

The new woman is essentially an independent labour unit whose energy is used not to serve the interests of a private family economy, but to perform socially useful and necessary labour. She is being liberated from those inner moral characteristics which marked the woman of the past. Female triviality, conservatism and restricted range of ideas, her envy and malice towards other women as rivals in the hunt for a provider – all these characteristics are no longer necessary in that sphere where she is now struggling to survive. As soon as the woman starts to live by her own work, she needs to develop different qualities and acquire new habits, and millions of working women throughout the world are hastening to morally re-arm themselves.

It is interesting to observe how, not only in our country but also abroad, women are learning to be efficient and workers whose labour is necessary. They are fully aware that their own well-being, and often also the existence of their children, depends directly on them, on their work and qualifications. Externally and internally they are adapting to the new conditions in which they live. Internally, psychologically, they are ceasing to be those patient, obedient beings who gave themselves wholly to husband and family. Now women have no time to be 'sentimental', and even less can they be 'obedient' and patient. It is more important that they be sure of their own strength, resolute in their actions, and not distracted by their emotions. . . .

In addition to their efficiency and their attempts, by raising their *qualifications* and improving their *health* and physical strength, to increase their value on the labour market, the new working women differ from the women of the past also in their strong feelings for and consciousness of their links with their class, with the collective. Women are involved in politics and, once again, if war drew large numbers of women into the political struggle, it was only the October Revolution which recognized publicly, by its laws, by the entire practice of the new Soviet system, that once the woman is working in and for society, she should be recognized as an active citizen. The enormous shift in the position of women in the Soviet Union has encouraged contending social groups to attempt to draw women onto their side. Everywhere, in every country, the political activity of women has shown unprecedented growth over the last ten years. Women are becoming members of government (Bang in Denmark – minister of education; Margaret Bondfield in the Ramsay MacDonald cabinet in Britain), they are entering the diplomatic corps and becoming the inspirational force behind major revolutionary movements (as for example Sun Tsin-lin, the wife of Sun Yat-sen). Women are learning to head departments, to take charge of economic organizations, to guide policy.

Would this have been possible without the Great October Revolution? Could the new woman-citizen and socially useful worker have emerged without the great whirlwind that blew across the world? Could the working women of other countries have taken such giant strides towards their own comprehensive emancipation without the October Revolution? Anyone who pauses to think realizes that the answer is clearly no. This is why working women

**121**

throughout the world cannot but feel that this tenth anniversary of the October Revolution is the great festival of workers of the world.

The October Revolution affirmed the importance of working women. The October Revolution has created those conditions which will ensure victory for the 'new woman'.

# PART 3

# AUTOBIOGRAPHY

# THE AIMS AND WORTH OF MY LIFE

Nothing is more difficult than writing an autobiography.[1] What should be emphasized? Just what is of general interest? It is advisable, above all, to write honestly and dispense with any of the conventional introductory protestations of modesty. For if one is called upon to tell about one's life so as to make the events that made it what it became useful to the general public, it can mean only that one must have already wrought something positive in life, *accomplished a task that people recognize*.[2] Accordingly it is a matter of forgetting that one is writing about oneself, of making an effort to abjure one's ego so as to give an account, as objectively as possible, of one's life in the making and of one's accomplishments. I intend to make this effort but whether it will turn out successfully is something else again. At the same time I must confess that, in a certain sense, this autobiography poses a problem for me. For by looking back while prying, simultaneously, into the future, I will also be presenting to myself the most crucial turning points of my being and accomplishments. *In this way I*[3] *may succeed in setting into bold relief that which concerns the women's liberation struggle and, further, the social significance which it has.*[4] That I ought not to shape my life according to the given model, that I would have to grow beyond myself in order to be able to discern my life's true line of vision was an awareness that was mine already in my

[1] Kollontai wrote this text in 1926. The English edition, translated by Salvator Attansio, was published in 1971. The text here re-incorporates sections from the galleys that had been crossed off – for one reason or another.
[2] Author's correction: created something which is recognized by society.
[3] perhaps
[4] Author's correction: to emphasize that which has an importance for the solution of the social problems of our time, and which also includes the great problem of complete women's liberation. Author's note with respect to 2: delete

youngest years. *At the same time I was also aware*[5] that in this way I could help my sisters to shape their lives, in accordance not with the given traditions but with their own free choice to the extent, of course, that social and economic circumstances permit. I always believed that the time inevitably must come when woman will be judged by the same moral standards applied to man. *For it is not her specific feminine virtue that gives her a place of honor in human society, but the worth of the useful mission accomplished by her,*[6] *the worth of her personality as human being, as citizen,*[7] *as thinker, as fighter. Subconsciously this motive was the leading force of my whole life and activity. To go my way, to work, to struggle, to create side by side with men,* and to strive for the attainment of a universal human goal*[8] (for nearly thirty years, indeed, I have belonged to the[9] Communists) *but, at the same time, to shape my personal, intimate life as a woman according to my own will* and according to the given laws of my nature.[10] *It was this that conditioned my line of vision.*[11] *And*[12] *in fact I have*[13] *succeeded in structuring my intimate life according to my own standards and I make no secret of my love experiences*[14] *any more than does a man.*[15] *Above all, however, I never let my feelings, the joy or pain of love take the first place in my life inasmuch as creativity, activity, struggle always occupied the foreground.* I managed to become a member of a government cabinet, of the first Bolshevik cabinet in the years 1917/18. I am also the first woman ever to have been appointed ambassadress, a post which I occupied for three years and from which I resigned

[5] Author's correction: I had a certain presentiment
[6] for society
[7] as creative worker
[8] who fought for the realization of our social ideals
[9] Socialists – now communists
[10] crossed out
[11] world-view
[12] I believe
[13] always
[14] when once love came, I have my relations to the man
[15] as men do

of my own free will.[16] *This may serve to prove that woman certainly can stand above the conventional conditions of the age. The World War, the stormy, revolutionary spirit now prevalent in the world in all areas has greatly contributed to blunting the edge of the unhealthy, overheated double standard of morality. We are already accustomed not to make overly taxing demands, for example,[17] on actresses and women belonging to the free professions in matters relating to their married life. Diplomacy, however, is a caste which more than any other maintains its old customs, usages, traditions, and, above all, its strict ceremonial. The fact that a woman, a 'free', a single woman was recognized in this position without opposition shows that the time has come when all human beings will be equally appraised according to their activity and their general human dignity. When I was appointed as Russian envoy to Oslo, I realized that I had thereby achieved a victory* not only for myself, but[18] *for women* in general[19] *and indeed, a victory over their worst enemy, that is to say,[20] over conventional morality and conservative concepts of marriage. When on occasion I am told that it is truly remarkable[21] that a woman has been appointed to such a responsible position, I always[22] think to myself that in the final analysis, the principal victory as regards women's liberation does not lie in this fact alone.* Rather, *what is of a wholly special significance here is that a woman,* like myself,[23] *who has settled scores with the double standard and* who has never concealed it,[24] *was accepted into a caste which to this very day staunchly upholds tradition and pseudo-*

---

[16] As was shown later, my private life, which I did not shape according to the traditional model, was no hindrance when in all seriousness it was a question of utilizing my energies for a new State [the Soviet Republic] and of functioning first as a member of the first Soviet cabinet, later as ambassadress.
[17] for example (crossed out)
[18] crossed out
[19] crossed out
[20] the
[21] 'truly remarkable' (in quotes)
[22] privately
[23] crossed out
[24] crossed out

morality. *Thus the example of my life can also serve to dispel*[25] *the*[26] *old goblin of the double standard also from the lives of other women.* And this *is a most crucial point of my own existence, which has a certain social-psychological worth* and contributes to the liberation struggle of working women. To avoid any misunderstanding, however, it should be said here that I am still far from being the type of the positively new women who take their experience as females with a relative lightness and, one could say, with an enviable superficiality, whose feelings and mental energies are directed upon all *other things*[27] in life but *sentimental love feelings.*[28] After all I still belong to the generation of women who grew up at a turning point in history. Love with its many disappointments, with its tragedies and eternal demands for perfect happiness[29] still played a very great role in my life. An all-too-great role! It was an expenditure of precious time and energy, fruitless and, in the final analysis, utterly worthless. We, the women of the past generation, did not yet[30] understand how to be free. The whole thing was an absolutely incredible squandering of our mental energy, a diminution of our labor power which was dissipated in barren emotional experiences. It is certainly true that

[25] can be dispelled (and crossed out)
[26] that
Author's note with respect to 4: delete completely
Author's new note: Instead of deleting
For it is not her specific womanish virtue that gives her a place of honour in human society, but the worth of her useful work accomplished for society, the worth of her personality as human being, as creative worker, as citizen, thinker, or fighter. To go my way, to create, to fight side by side with men for the realization of our social ideals (indeed for almost thirty years I belonged to the communists), but, at the same time, to shape my personal life as a woman according to my will. Subconsciously this was the guiding force of my whole life and activity Above all, however, I never let my feelings, joy in love, or sorrow take the first place in my life: productive work, activity, struggle always stood in the foreground.
[27] Author's correction: primarily upon all other areas
[28] Author's correction: and are not guided by sentimental love-feelings
[29] Author's correction: 'spiritual community'
[30] Author's correction: inwardly, in the mind

we, myself as well as many other activists, militants and working women contemporaries, were able to understand that love was not the main goal of our life and that we knew how to place work at its centre. Nevertheless we would have been able to create and achieve much more had our energies not been fragmentized in the eternal struggle with *our egos and with*[31] our feelings for another. It was, in fact, an eternal defensive war against the intervention of the male into our ego, a struggle revolving around the problem-complex: work or marriage and love? We, the older generation, did not yet understand, as most men do and as young women are learning today, that work and the longing for love can be harmoniously combined *so that work remains as the main goal of existence.*[32] Our mistake was that each time we succumbed to the belief that we had finally found the one and only in the man we loved, the person with whom we believed we could blend our soul, one who was ready fully to recognize us as a spiritual-physical force.[33]

But *over and over again things turned out differently, since*[34] the man always tried to impose his ego upon us and adapt us fully to his purposes. Thus despite everything the inevitable inner rebellion ensued, over and over again since love became a fetter. We felt enslaved and tried to loosen the love-bond. And after the eternally recurring struggle with the beloved man, we finally tore ourselves away and rushed toward freedom. Thereupon we were *again*[35] alone, *unhappy,*[36] lonesome, but free – free to pursue our beloved, chosen ideal – work.

Fortunately young people, the present generation, no longer have to go through this kind of struggle which is absolutely unnecessary to human society. Their abilities, their work-energy

[31] crossed out
[32] so that only a very subordinate place remains available to love
[33] Author's correction: unreservedly gave our entire ego to the beloved man in the hope that thereby we could attain a complete spiritual harmony.
[34] crossed out
[35] crossed out
[36] crossed out

will be reserved for their creative activity. *Thus the existence of barriers will become a spur.*[37]

It is essential that I relate some details here about my private life. My childhood was a very happy one, judging by outward circumstances. My parents belonged to the *old* Russian nobility.[38] I was the only child born of my mother's second marriage (mother was separated and I was born outside the second marriage, and then adopted). I was the youngest, the most spoiled, and the most coddled member of the family. This, perhaps, was the root cause of the protest against everything around me that very early burgeoned within me. Too much was done for me in order to make me happy. I had no freedom of maneuver either in the children's games I played or in the desires that I wanted to express. At the same time *I wanted to be free.*[39] I wanted to express desires on my own, to shape my own little life. My parents were well-to-do. There was no luxury in the house, but I did not know the meaning of privation. Yet I saw how other children were forced to give up things, and I was particularly and painfully shocked by the little peasant children who were my playmates (we lived almost always in the countryside, on the estate of my grandfather, who was a Finn). Already as a *small*[40] child I criticized[41] the injustice of adults and *I experienced as a blatant* contradiction[42] the fact that everything was offered to me whereas so much was denied to the other children. *My criticism sharpened as the years went by and the feeling of revolt against the many proofs of love around me grew apace.*[43] Already early in life I had eyes for the social injustices prevailing in Russia. I was never sent to school because my parents lived in a constant state of anxiety over my health and they could not endure

[37] crossed out
[38] Author's correction: old Russian landowner (class)
[39] crossed out
[40] Author's correction: experienced
[41] crossed out
[42] Author's correction: painfully felt the
[43] crossed out

the thought that I, like all other children, should spend two hours daily far from home. My mother probably also had a certain horror of the liberal influences with which I might come into contact at the high school. Mother, of course, considered that I was already sufficiently critically[44] inclined. Thus I received my education at home under the direction of a proficient, clever tutoress who was connected with Russian revolutionary circles. I owe very much to her, Mme. Marie Strakhova. I took[45] the examinations qualifying me for admission to the university when I was barely sixteen *(in 1888)*[46] and thereafter I was expected to lead the life of a 'young society woman'.[47] Although my education had been unusual and caused me much harm (for years I was extremely shy and utterly inept in the practical matters of life), it must nevertheless be said that my parents were by no means reactionaries. On the contrary, they were even[48] rather progressive for their time. But they held fast to traditions where it concerned the child, the young person under their roof. My first bitter struggle against these traditions revolved around the idea of marriage. I was supposed to make a *good match*[49] and mother was bent upon marrying me off at a very early age. My oldest sister, at the age of nineteen, had contracted marriage with a highly placed gentleman who was nearly *seventy*.[50] I revolted against this *marriage of convenience*, this marriage for money[51] and wanted to marry only for love, *out of a great passion*.[52] Still very young, and against my parents' wishes, I chose my cousin, an impecunious young engineer whose name, Kollontai, I still bear

---

[44] Author's correction: 'rebelliously'
[45] Author's correction: in St. Petersburg
[46] crossed out
[47] crossed out
[48] Author's correction: liberal
[49] Author's correction: 'good match' (in quotes)
[50] Author's correction: sixty
[51] Author's correction: 'marriage of convenience' and 'marriage for money' (in quotes)
[52] "great passion" (in quotes)

today. My maiden name was Domontovich. The happiness of my marriage lasted hardly three years. I gave birth to a son. Although I personally raised my child with *great care*,[53] motherhood was never the kernel of my existence. A child had not been able to draw the bonds of my marriage tighter. I still loved my husband, but the happy life of a housewife and spouse became for me a 'cage'. More and more my *sympathies, my*[54] interests turned to the revolutionary working class of Russia. I read voraciously. I zealously studied *all*[55] social questions, attended lectures, and worked in semi-legal societies for the enlightenment of the people. These were the years of the flowering of Marxism in Russia (1893-96). Lenin at that time was only a novice in the literary and revolutionary arena. George Plekhanov was the leading mind of the time. I stood close to the materialist conception of history, since in early womanhood I had inclined towards the realistic school. I was an enthusiastic follower of Darwin and Roelsches. A visit to the big and famous Krengolm textile factory, which employed 12,000 workers of both sexes, decided my fate. I could not lead a happy, peaceful life when the working population was so terribly enslaved. I simply had to join this movement. At that time this led to differences with my husband, who felt that my inclinations constituted an act of personal defiance directed against him. I left husband and child and journeyed to Zurich in order to study political economy under Professor Heinrich Herkner. Therewith[56] began my conscious life on behalf of the revolutionary goals of the working-class movement. When I came back to St. Petersburg – now Leningrad – in 1899, I joined the illegal Russian Social Democratic Party. I worked as a writer and propagandist. The fate of Finland, whose independence and relative freedom were being threatened by the reactionary policy of the Tsarist regime at the end of the '90s, exercised a

[53] crossed out
[54] crossed out
[55] Author's correction: the
[56] Author's correction: at that time; second correction: then

wholly special power of attraction upon me. Perhaps my particular gravitation towards Finland resulted from the impressions I received on my grandfather's estate during my childhood. I actively espoused the cause of Finland's national liberation. Thus my first *extensive*[57] scientific work in political economy was a *comprehensive investigation*[58] of the living and working conditions of the Finnish proletariat *in relation to industry.*[59] The book appeared in 1903 in St. Petersburg. My parents had just died, my husband and I had been living separately for a long time, and only my son remained in my care. Now I had the opportunity to devote myself completely to my *aims:*[60] to the Russian revolutionary movement and to the working-class movement *of the whole world.*[61] Love, marriage, family, all were secondary, transient matters. They were there, they intertwine with my life over and over again. But as great as was my love for my husband, immediately it transgressed a certain limit in relation to my feminine proneness to make sacrifice, rebellion flared in me anew. I had to go away, I had to break with the man of my choice, otherwise (this was a subconscious feeling in me) I would have exposed myself to the danger of losing my selfhood. It must also be said that not a single one of the men who were close to me has ever had a direction-giving influence on my inclinations, strivings, or my world-view. On the contrary, most of the time I was the guiding spirit. I acquired my view of life, my political line from life itself, and in uninterrupted study *from*[62] books.

In 1905, at the time the so-called first revolution in Russia broke out, after the famous Bloody Sunday, I had already acquired a reputation in the field of economic and social literature. And in those stirring times, when all energies were utilized in the storm of

---

[57] Author's correction: more comprehensive [in German grosse, grossere – tr.]
[58] Author's correction: studies on the
[59] crossed out
[60] Author's correction: to my work
[61] crossed out
[62] Author's correction: and

revolt, it turned out that I had become very popular as an orator. Yet in that period *I realized for the first time how little our Party concerned itself with the fate of the women of the working class and how meager was its interest in women's liberation. To be sure a very strong bourgeois women's movement was already in existence in Russia. But my Marxist outlook pointed out to me with an illuminating clarity that* women's liberation[63] could take place only as the result of the victory of a new social order and a different economic system. Therefore I threw myself into the struggle between the Russian[64] suffragettes and strove with all my might to induce the working-class movement to include the woman question as one of the aims of its struggle *in its programme.*[65] It was very *difficult*[66] to win my fellow *members*[67] over to this idea. I was completely isolated with my ideas and demands. Nevertheless in the years 1906-1908 I won a small group of women Party comrades over to my plans. I[68] wrote[69] an article published in the illegal press in 1906 in which *for the first time*[70] I set forth the demand to call the working-class movement into being in Russia through systematic Party work. In autumn of 1907 we opened up the first Working Women's Club. Many of the members of this club, who were still very young workers at that time, now occupy important posts in the new Russia and in the Russian Communist Party (K. Nicolaieva, Marie Burke, etc.). One result of my *activity in connection with the women workers,*[71] but especially

---

[63] Author's correction: I realized that in Russia little had yet been done to draw women workers into the liberation struggle. To be sure a quite strong bourgeois women's movement already existed in Russia at that time. But, as a Marxist, it was clear to me that the lib-

[64] Author's correction: against the bourgeois-minded

[65] crossed out

[66] Author's correction: not so easy

[67] Author's correction: comrades

[68] Author's correction: Since

[69] Author's correction: I

[70] crossed out

[71] Author's correction: and propaganda work among the masses of women-workers

of my political writings – among which was a pamphlet on Finland containing the call to rise up against *the Tsarist Duma*[72] with 'arms'– was the institution of legal proceedings against me which held out the grim prospect of spending many years in prison. I was forced to disappear immediately and was never again to see my home. My son was taken in by good friends, my small household liquidated. I became 'an illegal'. It was a time of strenuous work.

The first All-Russian Women's Congress which had been called by the bourgeois suffragettes was scheduled to take place in December of 1908. At that time the reaction was on the rise and the working-class movement was prostrate again after the first victory in 1905. Many Party comrades were in jail, others had fled abroad. The vehement struggle between the two factions of the Russian Workers Party broke out anew: the Bolsheviks on the one side, the Mensheviks on the other. *In 1908 I belonged to the Menshevik faction, having been forced thereto by the hostile position taken by the Bolsheviks towards the Duma, a pseudo-Parliament called by the Tsar in order to Pacify the rebellious spirits of the age. Although with the Mensheviks I espoused the point of view that even a pseudo-Parliament should be utilized as a tribute for our Party and that the elections for the Duma must be used as an assembling point for the working class. But I did not side with the Mensheviks on the question of coordinating the forces of the workers with the Liberals in order to accelerate the overthrow of absolutism. On this point I was, in fact, very left-radical and was even branded as a 'syndicalist' by my Party comrades.*[73] Given my attitude towards the Duma it logically followed that I considered it useless to exploit the first bourgeois women's congress in the interest of our Party. Nevertheless I worked with might and main to assure that *our*[74] women workers, who were to participate in the Congress, emerged as an independent and distinct group. I managed to carry out this plan but not without

[72] Author's correction: Tsarism
[73] Author's note: delete
[74] Author's correction: the

AUTOBIOGRAPHY

opposition. My Party comrades[75] accused me and those women-comrades who shared my views of being 'feminists' and of placing too much emphasis on matters of concern to women only. At the time there was still no comprehension *at all*[76] of the extraordinarily important role in the struggle devolving upon self-employed professional women. Nevertheless our will prevailed. A women-workers' group came forward at the Congress in St. Petersburg with its *own*[77] programme and it drew a clear line of demarcation between the bourgeois suffragettes and the women's liberation movement of the working class in Russia. However, I was forced to flee before the close of the Congress because the police had come upon my tracks. I managed to cross the frontier into Germany and thus, in December of 1908, began a new period of my life, political emigration.

[75] Author's correction: (the Mensheviks)
[76] Author's correction: insufficient
[77] Author's correction: the socialist

As a political refugee henceforth I lived in Europe and America until the overthrow of Tsarism in 1917. As soon as I arrived in Germany, after my flight, I joined the German Social Democratic Party in which I had many personal friends, among whom I especially numbered Karl Liebknecht,[1] Rosa Luxemburg, *Karl Kautsky*.[2] Clara Zetkin also had a great influence on my *activity*[3] in defining the principles of the women-workers' movement in Russia. Already in 1907 I had taken part, as a delegate from Russia, in the first International Conference of Socialist Women that was held in Stuttgart. This gathering was presided over by Clara Zetkin and it made an enormous contribution to the development of the women-workers' movement along Marxist lines. I put myself at the disposal of the Party press as a writer on social and political questions, and I was also frequently called upon as an orator by the German Party and I worked for the Party as an agitator from the Palatinate to Saxony, from Bremen to south Germany. But I assumed[4] no leading posts either in the Russian party or in the German party.[5] By and large I was mainly a 'popular orator' and an esteemed political writer. *I can now openly confess*[6] that in the Russian Party I deliberately kept somewhat aloof from the controlling centre, and that is explainable mainly by the fact that I was not yet in complete agreement with the policy of my comrades.[7] *But I had no desire to pass over to the Bolsheviks, nor could I for that matter since at the time it seemed to me as if they did not attach sufficient importance*

[1] Author's correction: And
[2] crossed out
[3] Author's correction: work
[4] Author's correction: at that time I had
[5] crossed out
[6] crossed out
[7] Author's correction: (the Mensheviks)

*to the development of the working-class movement in 'breadth and depth'. Therefore I worked on my own seemingly almost as though I wanted to remain in the background without setting my sights or obtaining a leading position.*[8] Here it must be admitted that, although I possessed a certain degree of ambition, like every other active human being, I was never animated by the desire to obtain 'a post'. For me 'what I am' was always of less importance than 'what I can', that is to say, what I was in a position to accomplish. In this way I, too, had my ambition and it was especially noticeable there where I stood *with my whole heart and soul*[9] in the struggle, where the issue was the abolition of the slavery of working women. I had above all set myself the task of winning over women workers in Russia to socialism and, at the same time, of working for the liberation of[10] woman, for her equality of rights. My book *The Social Foundations of the Women's Question* had appeared shortly before my flight; it was a polemical disputation with the bourgeois suffragettes but, at the same time, a challenge to the Party to build a viable women workers' movement in Russia. The book enjoyed great success. At that time I wrote for the legal and illegal press. Through an exchange of letters I tried to influence Party comrades and women workers themselves. *Naturally, I always did this in such a way that I demanded from the Party that it*[11] *espouse* the cause of women's liberation. I did not always have an easy time of it. Much passive resistance, little understanding, and even less interest for this aim, over and over again, lay as an obstacle in the path. It was not until 1914, shortly before the outbreak of the World War, that finally both factions – the Mensheviks and the Bolsheviks – took up the question in an earnest and practical way, a fact which had on me an effect almost tantamount to a personal commendation. Two periodicals for working women were launched in Russia; the

---

[8] Author's note: delete
[9] crossed out
[10] Author's correction: working
[11] Author's correction: a more zealous activity

International Working Women's Congress of March 8, 1914, was celebrated. I was still living in exile, however, and could help the so dearly loved women-workers' movement in my homeland only from afar. I was in close contact, also from afar, with the working women of Russia. Already several years earlier[12] I had been appointed by the Textile Workers' Union as an official delegate to the Second International Conference of Socialist Women (1910) and, *further*,[13] to the extraordinary International Socialist Congress in Basel in 1912. Later when a draft of a bill on social insurance was introduced in the Russian pseudo-Parliament (the Duma), the Social Democratic Duma faction (of the Menshevik wing) requested me to elaborate the draft of a bill on maternity welfare. It was not the first time that the[14] faction lay claim to my energies for legislative work. Just before I was forced to go into exile, I had been enlisted by them – as a qualified expert – to participate in the deliberation of the question of Finland in the Imperial Duma.

The task that had been assigned to me, namely, the elaboration of a draft of a bill in the field of maternity welfare, motivated me to undertake a most thorough study of this special question. The *Bund für Mutterschutz*, and the outstanding work of Dr. Helene Stöcker, also provided me with valuable suggestions. Nevertheless I also studied the question in England, France, and in the Scandinavian countries. The result of these studies was my book *Motherhood and Society*, a *comprehensive*[15] work of 600 pages on maternity welfare and the relevant legislation in Europe and Australia. The fundamental regulations and demands in this field, which I summed up at the end of my book, were realized later in 1917 by the Soviet regime in the first social insurance laws.

For me the years of political emigration were hectic, *quite*

---

[12] crossed out
[13] crossed out
[14] Author's correction: Duma
[15] Author's correction: a

*stirring*[16] years. I travelled as a Party orator from country to country. In 1911, in Paris, I organized the housewives' strike '*La grève des menagères*' against the high cost of living. In 1912 I worked in Belgium setting the groundwork for the miners' strike in the Borinage and in the same year the Party dispatched me to the left-oriented Socialist Youth Association of Sweden in order to strengthen the Party's[17] anti-militaristic tendencies. Several years earlier, *this still merits mention here,*[18] I fought in the ranks of the British Socialist Party side by side with Dora Montefiore *and Madame Koeltsch*[19] against the English suffragettes for the strengthening of the still fledgling socialist working-women's movement. In 1913 I was again in England. This time I was there in order to take an active part in a protest action against the famous 'Beilis Trial' which had been instigated by the anti-semites in Russia. In the spring of the same year, the left wing of the Swedish Social Democratic Party invited me to Sweden. These were truly hectic years, marked by the most varied types of militant activity. Notwithstanding, my Russian Party comrades also laid claim to my energies and appointed me delegate to the Socialist Party and Trade Union Congress. *Thus with the help of Karl Liebknecht I also sparked an activity in Germany on behalf of the deported socialist members of the Duma.*[20] In 1911 I was called to the Russian Party School in Bologna, where I delivered a series of lectures. The present Russian Minister of Education in Soviet Russia, A. Lunacharsky, Maxim Gorky, as well as the famous Russian economist and philosopher A. Bogdonov, were the founders of this Party school, and Trotsky delivered lectures at the school at the same time that I was there. The present Soviet Russian Minister of Foreign Affairs, G. Chicherin, who at that time worked as secretary of a relief agency for political

---

[16] crossed out
[17] Author's correction: in Sweden
[18] crossed out
[19] crossed out
[20] Author's note: delete

refugees, oftentimes called upon me to hold public lectures on the most disparate cultural problems of Russian life in order to help fill the relief agency's almost empty kitty. At his behest I travelled all over Europe but Berlin was my fixed abode. I felt at home in Germany and have always greatly appreciated the conditions there so ideally suited for scientific work. But I was not allowed to give speeches in Prussia. On the contrary, I had to keep as quiet as possible to avoid expulsion by the Prussian police.

Then the World War broke out and once again I arrived at a new turning point in my life.

*But before I talk about this important period of my intellectual existence, I still want to say a few words about my personal life. The question arises whether in the middle of all these manifold, exciting labours and Party-assignments I could still find time for intimate experiences, for the pangs and joys of love. Unfortunately, yes! I say unfortunately because ordinarily these experiences entailed all too many cares, disappointments, and pain, and because all too many energies were pointlessly consumed through them. Yet the longing to be understood by a man down to the deepest, most secret recesses of one's soul, to be recognized by him as a striving human being, repeatedly decided matters. And repeatedly disappointment ensued all too swiftly, since the friend saw in me only the feminine element which he tried to mould into a willing sounding board to his own ego. So repeatedly the moment inevitably arrived in which I had to shake off the chains of community with an aching heart but with a sovereign, uninfluenced will. Then I was again alone. But the greater the demands life made upon me, the more the responsible work waiting to be tackled, the greater grew the longing to be enveloped by love, warmth, understanding. All the easier, consequently, began the old story of disappointment in love, the old story of Titania in* A Midsummer Night's Dream.[21]

The outbreak of the World War found me in Germany. My son

---

[21] Author's note: delete

was with me. We were both arrested because my identity papers were not in order. During the house search, however, the police found a mandate from the Russian Social Democratic Party appointing me as delegate to the World Congress of Socialists. Suddenly the gentlemen from Alexander Platz became utterly charming: they figured that a female Social Democrat could not be a friend of the Tsar *and consequently certainly not an enemy of Germany. They were right.*[22] I was in fact no enemy of Germany and still less a Russian patriot. To me the war was an abomination, a madness, a crime, and from the first moment onwards – more out of impulse than reflection – I inwardly rejected it and could never reconcile myself with it *up to this very moment.*[23] The intoxication of patriotic feelings has always been something alien to me, on the contrary I felt an aversion for everything that smacked of super-patriotism. I found no understanding for my 'anti-patriotic' attitude among my own *Russian*[24] Party comrades, *who also lived in Germany.*[25] Only Karl Liebknecht, his wife Sofie Liebknecht, and a few other German Party comrades, like myself, espoused the same standpoint and, *like myself,*[26] considered it a socialist's duty to struggle against the war. Strange to say, I was present in the Reichstag on August 4, the day the war budget was being voted on. The collapse of the German Socialist Party struck me as a calamity without parallel. I felt utterly alone and found comfort only in the company of the Liebknechts.

With the help of some German Party friends I was able to leave Germany with my son in August of 1914 and emigrate to the Scandinavian peninsula. I left Germany not because I had felt the slightest manifestation of unfriendliness towards me but only for the reason that without a sphere of activity I would have been forced to live in idleness in that country. I was impatient to take

---

[22] crossed out
[23] crossed out
[24] crossed out
[25] Author's correction: at that time
[26] crossed out

up the struggle against the war. After arriving on Sweden's neutral soil, I *immediately*[27] began the work against the war *and for*[28] *the* international solidarity of the world working class. An appeal to working women made its way, along illegal channels, to Russia and to different other countries. In Sweden I wrote and spoke against the war. I spoke at public meetings, most of which had been called by the leftist-leaning *world-famous*[29] Swedish Party leaders Zeta Höglund and Frederic Strön. I found in them the pure echo of my *ideas and*[30] feelings and we joined forces in a common task for the victory of internationalism and against the war hysteria. It was only later that I learned of the attitude which the leading minds of the Russian Party had taken towards the war. When the news finally reached us, by way of Paris and Switzerland, it was for us a day of ineffable joy. We received assurance that both Trotsky and Lenin, although they[31] belonged to different factions of the Party, had militantly risen up against the war. Thus I was no longer 'isolated'. *A new grouping was proposed*[32] in the Party, the internationalists and the 'social-patriots'. *A Party periodical was also founded in Paris.*[33] In the middle of my zealous activities, however, I was arrested by the Swedish authorities and brought to the Kungsholm prison. The worst moment during this arrest was born of my concern over the identity papers of a good friend and Party comrade, Alexander Shlyapnikov, who had just arrived illegally in Sweden from Russia, which I had taken over for safe-keeping. Under the eyes of the police I managed to hide them under my blouse and somehow make them disappear. Later I was transferred from the Kungsholm prison to the prison in Malma and then banished to Denmark. As far as I know I was one of the first of the European socialists to

---

[27] crossed out
[28] Author's correction: through revival of the
[29] crossed out
[30] crossed out
[31] Author's correction: both
[32] Author's correction: a new grouping took place
[33] crossed out

be jailed because of anti-war propaganda. *In Denmark I continued my work but with greater prudence. Nevertheless*[34] the Danish police did not leave me in peace. Nor did the Danish Social Democrats exhibit friendliness for the internationalists. In February of 1915 I emigrated to Norway where together with Alexander Shlyapnikov we served as a link between Switzerland, the place of residence of Lenin and of the Central Committee,[35] and Russia. We had full contact with the Norwegian socialists. On March 8 of the same year I tried to organize an international working women's demonstration against the war in Christiania (now Oslo), but the representatives from the belligerent countries did not show up.

That was the time when the decisive rupture in Social Democracy was being prepared, since the patriotically minded socialists could not go along with the internationalists. Since the Bolsheviks were those who most consistently fought social-patriotism, in June of 1915 I officially joined the Bolsheviks *and entered into a lively correspondence with Lenin (Lenin's letters to me have recently been published in Russia).*[36]

I again began to do a prodigious amount of writing, this time for the international-minded press of the most different countries: England, Norway, Sweden, America, Russia. At this time one of my pamphlets, *Who Profits from the War?*, appeared. Deliberately written in a very popular view, it was disseminated in countless editions, *in millions of copies,*[37] and was translated into several languages, German included. So long as the war continued, the problem of women's liberation obviously had to recede into the background since *my only concern, my highest aim,*[38] was to fight against the war and call a new Workers' International into being. In the autumn of 1915 the German section of the American Socialist

[34] crossed out
[35] Author's correction: of our Party
[36] crossed out
[37] crossed out
[38] Author's correction: our only and living aim

Party invited me to journey to America to deliver lectures there in the spirit of 'Zimmerwald' (a gathering of international-minded socialists). I was immediately ready to cross the ocean for this purpose, despite the fact that my friends determinedly advised me against it. They were all deeply worried about me because the journey had become very hazardous as a result of submarine warfare. But the aim enticed me enormously. My propaganda tour in America lasted five months, during which time *I visited eighty-one cities in the United States and delivered lectures in German, French, and Russian.*[39] The work was extremely strenuous, *but also as fruitful, and I had warrant to believe that as a result the internationalists in the American Party were strengthened. Much opposition to the war, passionate debates, also existed overseas, but the police did not bother me.*[40] The newspapers, by turns, branded me either as a spy of the German Kaiser or as an agent of the Entente. I returned to Norway in the spring of 1916. I love Norway with its incomparable fjords and its majestic mountains, its courageous, gifted, and industrious people. At that time I lived on the famous Holmenkollen near Oslo and continued to work with the view 'of welding together all the forces of the internationalists' in opposition to the World War. *I shared Lenin's view which aimed at spreading the conviction that the war could be defeated only by the Revolution, by the uprising of the workers. I was in substantial agreement with Lenin and stood much closer to him than many of his older followers and friends.*[41] But my sojourn in Norway was not a long one because only a few months after my arrival I had to embark upon a second journey to America, where I remained till shortly before the outbreak of the Russian Revolution. *For me the situation in America had changed insofar as, in the meanwhile, many Russian Party comrades had come over,*

---

[39] Author's correction: I had to cross the whole of the United States from the Atlantic to the Pacific Ocean and deliver lectures in the most different languages along the lines of the Internationalists

[40] Author's note: delete

[41] Author's note: delete

*Trotsky among others. We worked zealously for the new Workers' International but America's intervention in the war aggravated our activity.*[42]

I had already been in Norway for several weeks, when the Russian people rose up against absolutism and dethroned the Tsar. A festive mood reigned among all our political friends. But I harboured no illusions because I knew that the overthrow of the Tsar would be only the beginning of even more momentous events and difficult social struggles *so I hastened*[43] back to Russia in March 1917. I was one of the first political emigrants *who came*[44] back to the liberated homeland. Torneo, the tiny frontier town lying north of the Swedish-Finnish frontiers, through which I had to pass, was still in the grip of a cruel winter. A sleigh carried me across the river which marks the frontier. On Russian soil stood a soldier. A bright red ribbon fluttered on his chest. 'Your identity papers, please, citizenness!' 'I have none. I am a political refugee.' 'Your name?' I identified myself. A young officer was summoned. Yes, my name was on the list of political refugees who were to be freely admitted into the country by order of the Workers' and Soldiers' Soviet. The young officer helped me out of the sleigh and kissed my hand, almost reverently. I was standing on the republican soil of liberated Russia! Could that be possible? It was one of the happiest hours of my *whole*[45] life. Four months later, by order of the Kerensky regime (the Provisional Government), the same charming young officer placed me under arrest as a dangerous Bolshevik at the Torneo frontier station. . . . Such is life's irony.

---

[42] Author's note: delete
[43] Author's correction: as soon as the political amnesty was declared by the new Republic I hastened
[44] Author's correction: who had the luck to
[45] crossed out

So overwhelming was the rush of subsequent events that to this very day I really do not know what I should describe and emphasize: what have I accomplished, desired, achieved? Was there altogether an individual will at that time? Was it not only the omnipotent storm of the Revolution, the command of the active, awakened masses that determined our will and action? Was there altogether a single human being who would not have bowed to the general will? There were only masses of people, bound together in a bipartite will, which operated either for or against the Revolution, for or against ending the war, and which sided for or against the power of the Soviets. Looking back one perceives only a massive operation, struggle, and action. In reality there were no heroes or leaders. It was the people, the working people, in soldiers' uniform or in civilian attire, who controlled the situation and who recorded its will indelibly in the history of the country and mankind. It was a sultry summer, a crucial summer of the revolutionary flood-tide in 1917! At first the social storm raged only in the countryside, the peasants set fire to the 'nests of gentle folk'. In the cities the struggle that raged was between the advocates of a republican-bourgeois Russia and the socialist aspirations of the Bolsheviks. . . .

As I have previously stated, I belonged to the Bolsheviks. Thus immediately, from the first days onwards, I found an absolute enormous pile of work waiting for me. Once more the issue was to wage a struggle against the war, against coalescence with the liberal bourgeoisie, and for the power of the workers' councils, the Soviets. The natural consequence of this stand was that the bourgeois newspapers branded me as a 'mad female Bolshevik'. But this bothered me not at all. *My field of activity was immense, and my followers, factory workers and women-soldiers, numbered*

147

*thousands.*[1] At this time I was very popular, especially[2] as an orator,[3] and, at the same time, hated and viciously attacked by the bourgeois press. *Thus it was a stroke of luck that I was*[4] so weighed down with current work that I found hardly any time to read the attacks and slanders against me. The hate directed against me, allegedly because I had been in the pay of the German Kaiser for the purpose of weakening the Russian front, grew[5] to monstrous proportions.

One of the most burning questions of the day was the high cost of living and the growing scarcity of vital necessities. Thus the women of the poverty-stricken strata had an indescribably hard time of it. *Precisely this situation prepared the terrain in the Party for 'work with women' so that very soon we were able to accomplish useful work.*[6] Already in May of 1917 a weekly called *The Women Workers* made its debut. *I authored an appeal to women against the high cost of living and the war.*[7] The first mass meeting, packed with thousands of people,[8] that took place in Russia under the Provisional Government, was organized by us, by the Bolsheviks. Kerensky and his ministers made no secret of their hatred of me, the 'instigator of the spirit of disorganization' in the Army. One particular article of mine in *Pravda* in which I interceded for German prisoners of war unleashed a *veritable storm of*[9] indignation on the part of patriotic-minded circles. When in April Lenin delivered his famous programmatic speech within the frame of the Soviets, *I was the only one of his Party comrades who took the poor to support his*

---

[1] Author's note: delete

[2] crossed out

[3] Author's correction: with the workers, the soldiers, the working women and the women soldiers

[4] Author's correction: I, however, was

[5] Author's correction: grew among the non-Soviet minded strata

[6] Author's correction: This gave our Party occasion to initiate enlightenment and political work among working women

[7] crossed out

[8] Author's correction: under the slogan of international solidarity and against the war

[9] Author's correction: the

*theses. What hatred this particular act kindled against me!*[10] Often I had to jump off tramcars before people recognized me, since I had become a topical theme of the day and often bore personal witness to the most incredible abuse and lies directed against me. *I should like to cite a small example which can show how the enemy worked with might and main to defame me. At that time the newspapers hostile to me were already writing about the 'Kollontai party dresses' which particularly then was laughable because my trunk had been lost en route to Russia, so I always wore the one and the same dress. There was even a little street ballad that commented on Lenin and me in verse.*[11] There was also nothing extraordinary in the fact that, threatened as I was by irritated mobs, I was always protected from the worst only by the courageous intercession of my friends and Party comrades. Nevertheless I myself personally *experienced little*[12] of the hatred around me and, of course, there was also a great number of enthusiastic friends: the workers, the sailors, the soldiers *who were utterly devoted to me.*[13] Moreover, the number of *our followers*[14] grew from day to day. Already in April, I was a member of the Soviet executive which, in reality, was the guiding political body of the moment, to which I belonged as the only woman and over a long period. In May of 1917 I took part in the strike of women laundry workers who set forth the demand that all laundries be 'municipalized'. The struggle lasted six weeks. Nevertheless the principal demand of the women laundry workers remained unmet by the Kerensky regime.

At the end of June, I was sent by my Party to Stockholm as a delegate to an international consultation which was interrupted when news reached us of the July uprising against the Provisional

[10] Author's note: delete
[11] Author's note: delete
[12] Author's correction: did not worry at all
[13] crossed out
[14] Author's correction: of the Bolsheviks

Government and of the extremely harsh measures that the[15] government was taking against the Bolsheviks. Many of our leading Party comrades had already been arrested, others, including Lenin, had managed to escape and go into hiding. The Bolsheviks were accused of high treason and branded as spies of the German Kaiser. The uprising was brought to a standstill and the coalition regime retaliated against all those who had manifested sympathy for the Bolsheviks. I immediately decided to return to Russia, although my friends *and Party comrades*[16] considered this to be a risky undertaking. They wanted me to go to Sweden and await the course of events. Well-intentioned as these counsels were, *and correct as they also appeared to me later,*[17] I nevertheless could not heed them. I simply had to go back. Otherwise it would appear to me as an act of cowardice to take advantage of the privilege, that had become mine, of remaining wholly immune from the persecutions of the Provisional Government, when a great number of my political friends were sitting in jail. *Later I realized that, perhaps, I might have been able to be move useful to our cause from Sweden, but I was under the compulsion of the moment.*[18] By order of the Kerensky regime I was arrested on the border of Torneo and subjected to the most boorish treatment as a spy. . . . But the arrest itself proceeded quite theatrically: during the inspection of my passport I was requested to step into the commandant's office. I understood what that meant. A number of soldiers were standing in an enormous room, pressed close against each other. Two young officers were also present, one of them being the charming young man who had received me *so amiably*[19] four months previously. A *veritable*[20] silence prevailed in the room. The facial expression of

---

[15] Author's correction: Provisional (Kerensky)
[16] crossed out
[17] crossed out
[18] crossed out
[19] Author's correction: amicably
[20] Author's correction: strange

the first officer, Prince B., betrayed a great nervousness. Composed, I waited to see what would happen next. 'You are under arrest,' explained Prince B. 'So. Has the counter-revolution triumphed. Do we again have a monarchy?' 'No,' was the gruff reply. 'You are under arrest by order of the Provisional Government.' 'I have been expecting it. Please, let my suitcase be brought in, I don't want it to be lost.' 'But, of course. Lieutenant, the suitcase!' I saw how the officers heaved a sigh of relief, and how the soldiers left the room with displeasure writ large on their faces. Later I learned that my arrest had occasioned a protest among the soldiers who insisted upon witnessing the arrest. The officers, however, had feared that I might make a speech to the soldiers. 'In that case we would have been lost,' one of them told me afterwards.

I was forced to wait for the course of the investigation, like the other Bolsheviks, in a Petrograd prison, in strict isolation. The more incredibly the regime conducted itself towards the Bolsheviks, the more *their* influence grew.[21] The march of the White general Kornilov on Petrograd strengthened the most radical elements of the Revolution. The people demanded that the jailed Bolsheviks be freed. Kerensky, however, refused to free me and it was only by an order of the Soviet that I was released from jail upon payment of bail. But already on the next day, Kerensky's decree that I be placed under house arrest hung over me. Nevertheless I was given my full freedom of movement one month before the decisive struggle, the October Revolution in 1917. Again my work piled up. Now the groundwork was to be set for a systematic women-workers' movement. The first conference of women workers was to be called. It also took place and it coincided with the overthrow of the Provisional Government and the establishment of the Soviet Republic.

At that time I was a member of the highest Party body, the

[21] Author's correction: of Bolshevism

Central Committee, *and I voted for the policy of armed uprising.*[22] I was also a member of different Party representations in decisive Congresses and State institutions (the preliminary Parliament, the democratic Congress, etc.). Then came the great days of the October Revolution. Smolny became historic. The sleepless nights, the permanent sessions. And, finally, the stirring declarations. 'The Soviets take power!' 'The Soviets address an appeal to the peoples of the world to put an end to the war.' 'The land is socialized and belongs to the peasants!'

The Soviet Government was formed. I was appointed People's Commissar (Minister) of Social Welfare. I was the only woman in the cabinet *and the first woman in history*[23] who had ever been recognized as a member of a government. When one recalls the first months of the Workers' Government, months which were so rich in *magnificent illusions,*[24] plans,[25] ardent initiatives to improve life, to organize the world anew, months of the real romanticism of the Revolution, one would in fact like to write about all else save about one's self. I occupied the post of Minister of Social Welfare from October of 1917 *to March of 1918.*[26] It was not without opposition that I was received by the former officials of the Ministry. Most of them sabotaged us openly and simply did not show up for work. But precisely this office could not interrupt its work, come what may, since in itself it was an extraordinarily complicated operation. It included the whole welfare programme for the war-disabled, hence for hundreds of thousands of crippled soldiers and officers, the pension system in general, foundling homes, homes for the aged, orphanages, hospitals for the needy, the work-shops making artificial limbs, the administration of playing-card

[22] Author's correction: crossed out 34
[23] Author's correction: So far as I knew it was the first time in history that a woman
[24] Author's correction: great aims and
[25] Author's correction: in
[26] crossed out

factories (the manufacture of playing cards was a State monopoly), *the educational system,*[27] clinical hospitals for women.[28] In addition a whole series of educational institutes for young girls were also under the direction of this Ministry. One can easily imagine the enormous demands these tasks made upon a small group of people who, at the same time, were novices in State administration. In a clear awareness of these difficulties *I formed,*[29] immediately, an auxiliary council in which experts such as physicians, jurists, pedagogues were represented alongside the workers and the minor officials of the Ministry. The sacrifice, the energy with which the minor employees bore the burden of this difficult task was truly exemplary. It was not only a matter of keeping the work of the Ministry going, but also of initiating reforms and improvements. New, fresh forces replaced the sabotaging officers of the old regime. A new life stirred in the offices of the formerly highly conservative Ministry. Days of grueling work! And at night the sessions of the councils of the People's Commissars (of the cabinet) under Lenin's chairmanship. A small, modest room and only one secretary who recorded the resolutions which changed Russia's life to its bottommost foundations. *My first act*[30] as People's Commissar was[31] to compensate a small peasant for his requisitioned horse. Actually by no stretch of the imagination did this belong to the functions of my office. But the man was determined to receive compensation for his horse. He had travelled from his distant village to the capital and had knocked patiently on the doors of all the ministries. Always with no results! Then the Bolshevik revolution broke out. The man had heard that the Bolsheviks were in favour of the workers and peasants. So he went to the Smolny Institute, to Lenin, who had to pay out the compensation. I do not know how the conversation

---

[27] Author's correction: leper colonies
[28] Author's correction: etc.
[29] Author's correction: we formed
[30] Author's correction: my first day
[31] Author's correction: began as follows

between Lenin and the small peasant went. As a result of it, however, the man came to me with a small page torn from Lenin's notebook on which I was requested to settle the matter somehow since at the moment the People's Commissariat for Social Welfare had the greatest amount of cash at its disposal. The small peasant received his compensation.

*My main work as People's Commissar consisted in the following:*[32] by decree to improve the situation of the war-disabled, to abolish religious instruction in the schools for young girls which were under the Ministry (this was still before the general separation of Church and State), and to transfer priests to the civil service, to introduce the right of self-administration for pupils in the schools for girls, to reorganize the former orphanages into government Children's Homes *(no distinction was to be made between orphaned children and those who still had fathers and mothers)*,[33] to set up the first hostels for the needy and street-urchins, to convene a committee, composed *only*[34] of doctors, which was to be commissioned to elaborate[35] the free public health system for the whole country. In my opinion the most important accomplishment of the People's Commissariat, however, was the legal foundation of a Central Office for Maternity and Infant Welfare. The draft of the bill relating to this Central Office was signed by me in January of 1918. A second decree followed in which I[36] changed all maternity hospitals into free Homes for Maternity and Infant Care,[37] in order thereby to set the groundwork for a comprehensive government system of pre-natal care. I was greatly assisted in coping with these tasks by Dr. Korolef. We also planned a 'Pre-Natal Care Palace', a model home

---

[32] Author's correction: the most important achievements of our People's Commissariat (Ministry for Social Welfare) in the first months after the October Revolution were the following:

[33] crossed out

[34] crossed out

[35] Author's correction: to work out

[36] crossed out

[37] Author's correction: were

with an exhibition room in which courses for mothers would be held *and, among many other things,*[38] model day nurseries were also to be established.[39] We were just about completing preparations for such a facility in the building of a girls' boarding school at which formerly young girls of the nobility had been educated and which was still under the direction of a countess, when a fire destroyed our work, which had barely begun! Had the fire been set deliberately? . . . I was dragged out of bed in the middle of the night. I rushed to the scene of the fire; the beautiful exhibition room was totally ruined, as were all the other rooms. Only the huge name-plate 'Pre-Natal Care Palace' still hung over the entrance door.

My efforts to nationalize maternity and infant care set off a new wave of insane attacks against me. All kinds of lies were related[40] about the 'nationalization of women', *about my legislative proposals which assertedly ordained that little girls of 12 were to become mothers.* A special fury gripped the religious followers of the old regime when, *on my own authority (the cabinet later criticized me for this action),*[41] I transformed the famous Alexander Nevsky monastery into a home for war invalids. The monks resisted and a shooting fray ensued. The press again raised a loud hue and cry against *me*.[42] The Church organized street demonstrations *against my action*[43] and also pronounced 'anathema' against me. . . .

*I received countless threatening letters, but I never requested military protection. I always went out alone, unarmed and without any kind of a bodyguard. In fact I never gave a thought to any kind of danger, being all too engrossed in matters of an utterly different*

---

[38] crossed out
[39] Author's correction: etc.
[40] Author's correction: written in Russian, on laws which 'obligated' 12-year-old girls to become mothers and suchlike
[41] Author's correction: we
[42] Author's correction: our action
[43] crossed out

*character.*[44] In February of 1918 a first State delegation of the Soviets was sent to Sweden *in order to clarify different economic and political questions.*[45] As People's Commissar I headed this delegation. But our vessel was shipwrecked; we were saved by landing on the Aland Islands which belonged to Finland. At this very time the struggle between the Whites and the Reds in the country had reached its most crucial moment and the German Army was also making ready to wage war against Finland.

The White troops occupied the Aland Islands on the very evening of our shipwreck as we were seated at dinner in an inn of the city of Marieham, rejoicing over our rescue. We managed to escape thanks to the greatest determination and cunning, yet one of our group, a young[46] Finn, was captured and shot. We returned to Petrograd, where the evacuation of the capital was being prepared with feverish haste: German troops already stood before the gates of the city.

Now began a *dark time*[47] of my life which I cannot treat of here since the events are still too fresh in my mind. *But the day will also come when I will give an account of them.*[48]

*There were differences of opinion in the Party.*[49] I resigned from my post as People's Commissar *on the ground of total disagreement with the current policy. Little by little I was also relieved of all my other tasks. I again gave lectures and espoused my ideas on 'the new woman' and 'the new morality'.*[50] The Revolution was in full swing. The struggle was becoming increasingly irreconcilable and bloodier, *much of what was happening did not fit in with my outlook.*[51] But after

---

[44] Author's note: delete

[45] crossed out

[46] Author's correction: 'red' (in quotes)

[47] Author's correction: period

[48] crossed out

[49] crossed out: Author's correction: I

[50] Author's note: delete

[51] crossed out

all[52] there was still the unfinished task, women's liberation. Women, of course, had received all rights but in practice, of course, they still lived under the old yoke: without authority in family life, enslaved by a thousand menial household chores, bearing the whole burden of maternity, even the material cares, because many women now found life alone as a result of the war and other circumstances.

In the autumn of 1916 when I devoted all my energies to drawing up systematic guidelines for the liberation of working women in all areas, *I found a valuable support in the*[53] first President of the Soviets, Sverdlov, now dead.[54] Thus the first Congress of Women Workers and Women Peasants could be called as early as November of 1918; some 1,147 delegates were present. Thus the foundation was laid for methodical work in the whole country for the *liberation*[55] of the women of the working and the peasant classes. A flood of new work was waiting for me. The question now was one of drawing women into the people's kitchens and of educating them to devote their energies to children's homes and day-care centers, the school system, household reforms, and still many other pressing matters. The main thrust of all this activity was to implement, in fact, equal rights for women as a labour unit in the national economy and as a citizen in the political sphere and, of course, with the special proviso: maternity was to be appraised as a social function and therefore protected and provided for by the State.

Under the guidance of Dr. Lebedevo, the State institutes for pre-natal care also flourished then. At the same time, central officers were established in the whole country to deal with issues and tasks connected with women's liberation and to draw women into Soviet work.[56]

---

[52] Author's correction: also
[53] Author's correction: it was the
[54] Author's correction: who recognized the task of the political education of working women as a serious aim of the Party and helped us in our work
[55] Author's correction: emancipation
[56] Author's correction: to win them over to the new political system, to educate them politically

The Civil War in 1919 saddled me with new tasks. When the White troops tried to march north from south Russia, I was again sent to the Ukraine and to the Crimea where at first I served as chairwoman of the enlightenment department in the Army. Later, *up to the evacuation of the Soviet government,*[57] I was appointed People's Commissar of Enlightenment and Propaganda in the Ukrainian government. *I managed to send 400 women communists out of the threatened zone near Kiev with a special train. I did my most possible best for the communist women workers' movement also in the Ukraine.*[58]

A serious illness tore me away from the exciting work for months. Hardly having recovered – at that time I was in Moscow – I took over the direction of the Coordinating Office for Work among Women and again a new period of intensive, gruelling work began. A communist women's *newspaper*[59] was founded, conferences and congresses of women workers were convoked. The foundation was laid for work with the women of the East (Mohammedans). Two world conferences of communist women took place in Moscow. The law liberalizing abortion was put through and a number of regulations of benefit to women were introduced by our Coordinating Office and legally confirmed. *At this time I had to do more writing and speaking than ever before. . . .* [60] Our work received wholehearted support from Lenin. And Trotsky, although he was overburdened with military tasks, unfailingly and gladly appeared at our conferences. Energetic, gifted women, two of whom are no longer alive,[61] sacrificially devoted all their energies to the work of the Coordinating Office.

At the eighth Soviet Congress, as a member of the Soviet

---

[57] crossed out
[58] Author's note: delete
[59] Author's correction: periodical
[60] crossed out
[61] Author's correction: Inessa Armand, and Samoslova

executive (*now there were already several women on this body*[62]),
I proposed a motion that the Soviets in all areas contribute to the
creation of a consciousness of the struggle for equal rights for
women and, accordingly, to involve them in State and communal
work. I[63] managed to push the motion through and to get it accepted
but not without resistance. It was a great, an enduring victory.

A heated debate flared up when I published my thesis on the
new morality. *For our Soviet marriage law, separated from the Church
to be sure, is not essentially more progressive than the same laws that
after all exist in other progressive democratic countries. Marriage,
civil marriage and*[64] although the illegitimate child *was*[65] placed on
a legal par with the legitimate child,[66] in practice a great deal of
hypocrisy and injustice still exists in this area. When one speaks
of the 'immorality' which the Bolsheviks purportedly propagated,
it suffices to submit our marriage laws to a close scrutiny to note
that in the divorce question we are on a par with North America
whereas in the question of the illegitimate child we have *not yet
even*[67] progressed as far as the Norwegians.

The most radical wing of the Party was formed around this
question. My theses, my *sexual and moral*[68] views,[69] were bitterly
fought *by many Party comrades of both sexes:*[70] *as were still other
differences of opinion in the Party regarding political guiding
principles.*[71] Personal and family cares were added thereto and
thus months in 1922 went by without fruitful work. Then in the
autumn of 1922 came my official appointment to the legation of the

---

[62] crossed out
[63] Author's correction: we
[64] crossed out
[65] Author's correction: in Soviet Russia
[66] Author's correction: is
[67] Author's correction: only
[68] crossed out
[69] Author's correction: in the area of sexual morality
[70] crossed out
[71] crossed out

Russian Soviet representation in Norway. I really believed that this appointment would be purely formal and that therefore in Norway I would find time to devote to myself, to my literary activity. Things turned out quite differently. With the day of my entry into office in Norway I also entered upon a wholly new course of work in my life which drew upon all my energies to the highest degree. During my diplomatic activity, therefore, *I wrote only one article, The Winged Eros, which caused an extraordinarily great flutter. Added to this were three short novels, Paths of Love, which have been published by Malik-Verlag in Berlin.*[72] My book *The New Morality and the Working Class* and a socio-economic study, *The Condition of Women in the Evolution of Political Economy*, were written when I was still in Russia.

[72] Author's correction: wrote little: three short stories, 'F Love', my first attempt at short-story writing, a sociological 'Winged Eros', and other unimportant articles.

I took up my duties in Norway in October of 1922 and as early as 1923 the head of the legation went on holiday so that I had officially to conduct the affairs of the Soviet Republic for him. Soon thereafter, however, I was appointed as the representative of my country in his stead. Naturally this appointment created a great sensation since, after all, it was the first time in history that a woman was officially active as an 'ambassador'. The conservative press and especially the Russian 'White' press were outraged and tried to make a real monster of immorality and a bloody bogey out of me. Now especially a profusion of articles were written *about my 'horrid views' in relation to marriage and love. Nevertheless I must stress here that it was only the conservative press that gave me such an unfriendly reception in my new position. In*[1] all the social relations which I had during the three[2] years of my *work*[3] in Norway, I never once experienced the least trace of aversion or mistrust against woman's capabilities. To be sure, the healthy, democratic spirit of the Norwegian people greatly contributed to this. Thus the fact is to be confirmed that my work as official *Russian*[4] representative[5] in Norway was never, and in no wise, made difficult for the reason that I belonged 'to the weaker sex'. In connection with my position as ambassadress I also had to assume the duties of a Trade Plenipotentiary of the Russian governmental trade representation in Norway. Naturally both tasks in their special way were new to me. *Nevertheless I set myself the*[6] *task of effecting the* de jure

---

[1] Author's correction: that in
[2] Author's correction: and one half
[3] Author's correction: diplomatic activity
[4] crossed out
[5] Author's correction: the Soviet Republic
[6] Author's correction: The

recognition of Soviet Russia and of re-establishing normal trade relations between the two countries which had been broken by the war and the revolution.[7] The work began with great zeal and the most roseate hopes. A *splendid*[8] summer and an eventful winter marked the year of 1923! The newly resumed trade relations were in full swing: Russian corn and Norwegian herring and fish, Russian wood products and Norwegian paper and cellulose. On February 15, 1924, Norway in fact[9] recognized the U.S.S.R. *de jure*. I was appointed '*chargé d'affaires*' and officially introduced into the diplomatic corps. Now negotiations for a trade treaty between the two countries began. My life was as crammed with strenuous work and highly interesting experiences alike. *I*[10] had also to settle grave questions connected with the further development of trade and of shipping. After several months, in August of 1924, I was appointed '*Ministre Plenipotentiere*' and handed over my warrant to the king of Norway with the usual ceremonial. This, of course, gave the conservative press of all countries another occasion to spew their invectives upon me. After all, never before in all history had a woman been accepted as ambassador with the customary pomp and ceremony.

The trade agreement was concluded *in Moscow*[11] at the end of 1925 and in February *I countersigned the ratified treaty in Oslo with the president of the Norwegian cabinet, I. L. Mowickl*.[12]

The signing marked the successful accomplishment of my whole mission in Norway. I could hasten towards new goals and *for this reason*[13] I left my post in Norway.

If I have attained something in this world, it was not my personal qualities that originally brought this about. Rather my

---

[7] Author's correction: laid special claim on my energies
[8] Author's correction: laden with work
[9] Author's correction: (in fact) [in parentheses]
[10] Author's correction: we
[11] crossed out
[12] Author's correction: the trade agreement was ratified
[13] crossed out

achievements are only a symbol of the fact that woman, after all, is already on the march to general recognition. It is the drawing of millions of women into productive work, which was swiftly effected especially during the war and which thrust into the realm of possibility the fact that a woman could be advanced to the highest political and diplomatic positions. Nevertheless it is obvious that only a country of the future, such as the Soviet Union, can dare to confront woman without any prejudice, to appraise her only from the standpoint of her skills and talents, and, accordingly, to entrust her with responsible tasks. Only the fresh revolutionary storms were strong enough to sweep away hoary prejudices against woman and only the productive-working people is able to effect the complete equalization and liberation of woman by building a new society.

*As I now end this autobiography, I stand on the threshold of new missions and life is making new demands upon me.*[14]

*No matter what further tasks I shall be carrying out, it is perfectly clear to me that the complete liberation of the working woman and the creation of the foundation of a new sexual morality will always remain the highest aim of my activity, and of my life.*[15]

In July of 1926
Alexandra Kollontai

[14] Author's correction: and to be sent to Mexico as ambassadress of the Soviet Union

[15] Author's note: delete